STEVENS PASS
WILD SKY AREA

STEVENS PASS
WILD SKY AREA

Text by **Rick McGuire**
Photos by **Ira Spring**

THE MOUNTAINEERS BOOKS

Published by
The Mountaineers
1001 SW Klickitat Way, Suite 201
Seattle, WA 98134

Published simultaneously in Great Britain by Cordee, 3a DeMontfort Street, Leicester, England, LE1 7HD

Manufactured in the United States of America

Editor: Christine Clifton-Thornton
Cover and book design: The Mountaineers Books
Layout: Marge Mueller, Gray Mouse Graphics
Mapmaker: Gray Mouse Graphics
Unless otherwise noted, photographer: Bob and Ira Spring or Kirkendall/Spring
Cover photograph: *Lake Serene and 5979-foot Mount Index*
Frontispiece: *Deception Creek in Alpine Lakes Wilderness*

Library of Congress Cataloging-in-Publication Data
McGuire, Rick.
55 hikes around Stevens Pass : Wild Sky area / text by Rick McGuire ; photos by Ira Spring.— 1st ed.
p. cm.
Includes bibliographical references and index.
ISBN 0-89886-958-7 (alk. paper)
1. Hiking—Washington (State)—Stevens Pass—Guidebooks. 2. Stevens Pass (Wash.)—Guidebooks. 3. Hiking—Washington (State)—Wild Sky Wilderness—Guidebooks. 4. Wild Sky Wilderness (Wash.)—Guidebooks. I. Title: Fifty-five hikes around Stevens pass. II. Title.
GV199.42.W22S742 2003
917.97'5—dc21
2003013191

Printed on recycled paper

Ira and Pat Spring, early 1980s

Ira Spring

December 24, 1918–June 5, 2003

Ira Spring passed away the week of National Trails Day, just as the production of this book was completed. As with all his many books we have published over the past forty years, this is a project he envisioned to inspire hikers to get out and experience a magnificent expanse of outdoors—which just so happens to also be up for consideration for wilderness status. Ira has promoted "green-bonding" in all his ventures, believing strongly that once people become acquainted with the beauty of a wild area, they are more likely to become personally invested in preserving and protecting it. When the day comes that the "Wild Sky" becomes the "Wild Sky Wilderness Area," it will happen in no small part because of Ira's persistent, unrelenting leadership and devotion to the splendid pleasures of what lies ahead, around the next bend in the trail.

With appreciation—
The staff of The Mountaineers Books,
Helen Cherullo, Publisher
Christine Clifton-Thornton, Editor
Marge Mueller, Book Designer

CONTENTS

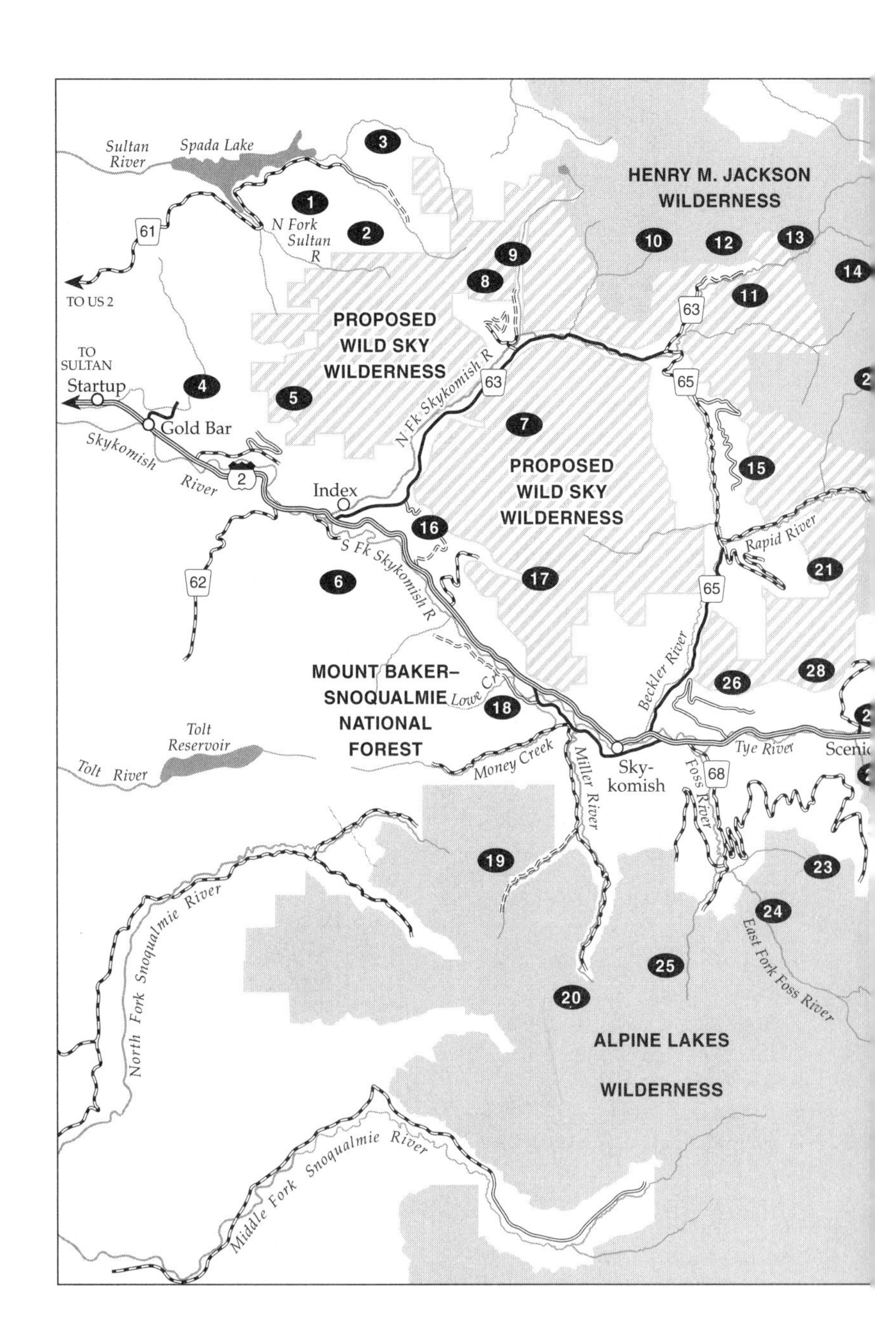
Sultan River
Spada Lake
HENRY M. JACKSON WILDERNESS
N Fork Sultan R
61
TO US 2
PROPOSED WILD SKY WILDERNESS
63
TO SULTAN
Startup
Gold Bar
65
Skykomish River
N Fk Skykomish R
PROPOSED WILD SKY WILDERNESS
2
Index
S Fk Skykomish R
Rapid River
62
65
MOUNT BAKER–SNOQUALMIE NATIONAL FOREST
Beckler River
Lowe Cr
Tolt Reservoir
Tolt River
Money Creek
Miller River
Sky-komish
Foss River
68
Tye River
North Fork Snoqualmie River
East Fork Foss River
ALPINE LAKES WILDERNESS
Middle Fork Snoqualmie River

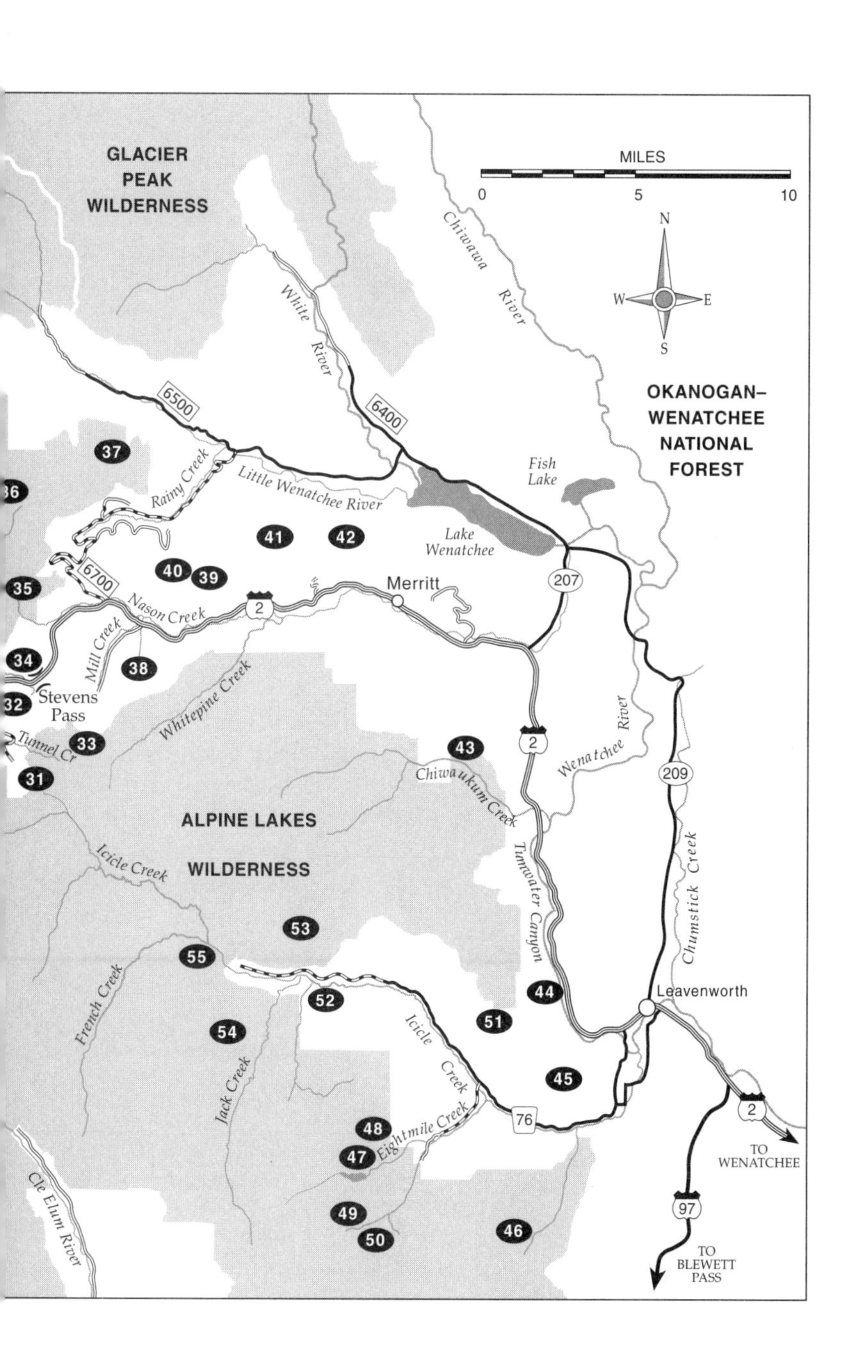
GLACIER PEAK WILDERNESS
MILES
0
5
10
N
W
E
S
OKANOGAN–WENATCHEE NATIONAL FOREST
ALPINE LAKES WILDERNESS
Chiwawa River
White River
6500
6400
6700
Rainy Creek
Little Wenatchee River
Fish Lake
Lake Wenatchee
Merritt
207
Nason Creek
2
Mill Creek
Stevens Pass
Tunnel Cr
Whitepine Creek
Wenatchee River
209
Chiwaukum Creek
Tumwater Canyon
Chumstick Creek
Icicle Creek
French Creek
Jack Creek
Eightmile Creek
Leavenworth
76
Cle Elum River
TO WENATCHEE
97
TO BLEWETT PASS
31
32
33
34
35
36
37
38
39
40
41
42
43
44
45
46
47
48
49
50
51
52
53
54
55

ACKNOWLEDGMENTS

The author would like to thank a few of the people who have helped to make this work possible. First and foremost, Mike Town, longtime explorer of the Skykomish country, for supplying much material, some of which originally appeared in the *Monroe Monitor*, one of the best small-town papers in Washington. Also Mark Lawler, the original Wild Sky Wilderness partisan, as well as, in no particular order, Don Parks, Harry Romberg, Norm Winn, Jon Owen, Tom Uniack, Jill Smith, Steve Higgins, Karen Fant, Kem Hunter, David Cameron, Conway Leovy, Jim Young, Bill Arthur, Jennifer Ekstrom, John Leary, Kristin Tremoulet, Rashmi Koushik, Sara McArdle, Greg Weiting, Bob Heirman, Kathy Johnson, Thom Peters, and others too numerous to mention, all of whom have contributed to protection of the Skykomish country in ways large and small. Thanks also to John Roper for supplying photographs, and to Kevin Geraghty for photographs and creation of a website, *www.wildsky.org*, where many color scenes of the Wild Sky country can be seen.

KEY TO MAP SYMBOLS

- highway
- railroad
- paved road
- gravel road
- dirt road
- primitive (walking) road
- trail
- cross-country route
- boundary (park or wilderness area)
- powerline
- ski lift
- 84 interstate highway
- 97 US highway
- 291 state highway
- 26 county highway
- 3060 national forest road
- 643 trail number
- TH trailhead
- ranger station
- building
- buildings in town
- campground
- backcountry campsite
- lookout
- radio tower
- mine
-)(pass
-][bridge
- gate
- spring
- river or stream
- waterfall
- lake
- marsh
- glacier

QUICK TRAIL FINDER

Number and name	Round-trip distance (miles)	Elevation gain (feet)	Difficulty	CHOOSE YOUR ATTRACTION											
				Alpine lakes, large and small	Riverside walks	Waterfalls, large and small	Salmon or steelhead in season	High-mountain, panoramic, or other views	Alpine meadows and flower fields	East-side springtime flowers	Impressive old growth or other forests	Fall colors	Solitude (maybe)	Bring the kids	Early season hikes (sometimes mid-winter)
1. Greider Lakes	6	2000	moderate	●									●		
2. Boulder Lake	8	2050	moderate	●										●	
3. North Fork Sultan	12	700	strenuous		●			●			●		●		
4. Wallace Falls	6	1250	moderate		●	●								●	●
5. Lake Isabel	6	2300	moderate	●		●									
6. Lake Serene	8	2000	strenuous	●		●					●				
7. Trout Creek	8	1400	moderate			●							●		
7. Iron Mountain	7	3400	strenuous		●								●		
8. Mineral Butte	12	3700	strenuous					●				●	●		
9. Silver Creek	7	800	easy	●		●									●
10. Blanca Lake	8	2700	strenuous	●				●			●	●	●		
11. West Cady Ridge	8	2200	moderate					●	●		●	●			
11. Bench Mark Mountain	16	3300	strenuous					●	●			●			
12. Curry Gap	10	1400	moderate								●				
12. Bald Eagle Trail	13	2700	strenuous					●	●			●			
13. North Fork Sky	8	700	easy		●						●			●	
13. Dishpan Gap	15	2600	strenuous		●			●	●						

CHOOSE YOUR ATTRACTION

Number and name	Round-trip distance (miles)	Elevation gain (feet)	Difficulty	Alpine lakes, large and small	Riverside walks	Waterfalls, large and small	Salmon or steelhead in season	High-mountain, panoramic, or other views	Alpine meadows and flower fields	East-side springtime flowers	Impressive old growth or other forests	Fall colors	Solitude (maybe)	Bring the kids	Early season hikes (sometimes mid-winter)
14. Cady Pass	10⅗	1300	moderate		●						●				
15. Evergreen Mtn	3	1300	moderate					●	●			●			
16. Heybrook Lookout	2½	1000	easy					●						●	●
17. Barclay Lake	4	300	easy	●				●					●		
17. Eagle Lake	8	1800	moderate	●				●				●			
18. Lowe Creek road	6	100	easy		●		●				●		●	●	●
19. West Fork Miller	9	1100	easy		●								●	●	
19. Coney Basin	7	1800	moderate		●										
20. Lake Dorothy	3	800	easy	●							●			●	
21. Scorpion Mtn	10	2600	strenuous					●	●						
22. Meadow Creek	14	2700	strenuous	●							●		●		
23. Tonga Ridge	6	500	easy					●	●			●		●	
24. East Fork Foss	10	500	easy		●				●		●			●	
24. Necklace Valley	18	3400	strenuous	●				●	●						
25. Trout Lake	3	360	easy	●			●				●			●	
25. Copper Lake	8	2300	moderate	●				●							
26. Beckler Peak	5	2000	strenuous					●					●		
27. Iron Goat Trail	6¾	800	easy					●				●		●	
28. Kelly Creek	9	2000	moderate					●			●		●		
29. Deception Creek	10	1150	moderate		●						●		●		

CHOOSE YOUR ATTRACTION

Number and name	Round-trip distance (miles)	Elevation gain (feet)	Difficulty	Alpine lakes, large and small	Riverside walks	Waterfalls, large and small	Salmon or steelhead in season	High-mountain, panoramic, or other views	Alpine meadows and flower fields	East-side springtime flowers	Impressive old growth or other forests	Fall colors	Solitude (maybe)	Bring the kids	Early season hikes (sometimes mid-winter)
30. Surprise Creek	10	2600	strenuous	●				●			●				
31. Hope & Mig Lakes	4	1660	modertae	●					●			●			
32. Grace Lakes	5	800	easy	●								●		●	
33. Josephine Lake	8	1770	moderate	●					●			●			
34. Skyline Lake	3	1050	easy	●				●				●		●	
35. Lake Valhalla: PCT	11	1900	moderate	●											
36. Lake Janus	7	1400	moderate	●				●							
37. Minotaur Lake	4	1750	strenuous	●				●	●			●			
38. Lanham Lake	3	1100	moderate	●									●		
39. Snowy Creek–Rock Mtn	9	3250	strenuous	●				●	●		●	●			
40. Rock Mtn–Rock Lake	11	4150	strenuous	●				●	●		●	●	●		
41. Merritt Lake	7	2000	moderate	●								●			
42. Alpine Lookout	12⅘	3500	strenuous					●	●			●			
43. Chiwaukum Creek	11	1500	moderate								●				
44. Tumwater Pipeline	2	100	easy		●		●			●					●
45. Icicle Ridge	3	1800	moderate					●		●		●			●
46. Snow Creek–Nada Lake	11	3600	strenuous	●											
47. Eightmile Lake	7	1360	moderate	●						●					
48. Lake Caroline	11	2900	strenuous	●				●	●	●		●			
49. Lake Stuart	10	1600	moderate	●				●							

CHOOSE YOUR ATTRACTION

Number and name	Round-trip distance (miles)	Elevation gain (feet)	Difficulty	Alpine lakes, large and small	Riverside walks	Waterfalls, large and small	Salmon or steelhead in season	High-mountain, panoramic, or other views	Alpine meadows and flower fields	East-side springtime flowers	Impressive old growth or other forests	Fall colors	Solitude (maybe)	Bring the kids	Early season hikes (sometimes mid-winter)
50. Colchuck Lake	9	2140	moderate	●				●							
51. Fourth of July Creek	4	2000	easy							●	●				
51. Fourth of July–Icicle	12	4800	strenuous					●	●	●					
52. Icicle Gorge	4	100	easy		●									●	
53. Chatter Creek	5	2500	moderate					●	●			●			
53. Lake Edna	11½	4500	strenuous	●				●	●			●			
54. Blackjack Ridge	6	3400	strenuous					●	●						
55. Icicle Creek	3	50	easy		●						●			●	
55. French Ridge	8	2900	strenuous					●	●						
Bonus Hikes															
1. Troublesome Creek	½	slight	easy		●	●	●				●				●
2. Bear Mountain View	½	250	easy					●			●		●		
3. Lake Elizabeth	7/10	none	easy	●							●	●	●	●	
4. Evans Lake	1	50	easy	●							●		●	●	
5. Deception Falls Nature Trail	½	slight	easy		●	●					●			●	●
6. Bygone Byways	½	50	easy		●						●	●		●	
7. Hidden Lake	1	350	easy	●							●			●	
8. Road 7903	1	500	easy							●	●	●	●		●
9. Castle Rock	½	400	easy							●	●	●			●
10. Peshastin Pinnacles	1½	450	easy							●		●		●	●

A LEGACY OF TRAILS

A Note From the Photographer

Newly opened buds of early spring flowers, fresh from winter's rain and chill; the fluttering green of leaves overhead, touched by brilliant sunshine deep in a summer forest; the earthy scent of autumn pine and the golden crunch of fallen leaves beneath well-worn hiking boots; crisp winter air made fresher still by the sight of snow along the frozen banks of a quiet mountain creek. The pleasures of hiking are made up of a thousand sensory moments, each as unique as the paths we take to experience the wilderness around us.

But where do those paths come from, and who works to keep them open? We all have a responsibility to help maintain the trails that lead to our favorite hiking destinations. But whether a mountain ridge or valley meadow, the work of creating a lasting trail, regardless of its destination, often begins far from the great outdoors.

On public lands, trails begin with the U.S. Forest Service. I have worked in conjunction with the Forest Service for more than forty years, talking to them about trails and listening to their perspective, and this is what I have learned: If you want to have an impact on the future of our trails, write a letter to the Forest Service. Tell them about your experiences on trails and let them know what needs improvement. I have seen a single letter influence the tide of reason in a Forest Service planning meeting—a letter written by someone like you—telling the Forest Service about how a trail to a fine destination could be made better or safer or longer, based on someone's personal experience on our public lands. Let the Forest Service know that your experience in the outdoors—*green-bonding* to the natural world—is valuable, a lasting impression that will only be available to future generations if we keep our trail systems healthy and growing.

The Forest Service listens to the public. Complaining about the actions of the Forest Service, when they are doing what the public wants, isn't the best choice; if you want to make a change, it is better to become part of the solution by suggesting what can be done rather than complaining about what has already been accomplished. I find that encouraging the Forest Service works wonders, whereas railing against their inadequacies is ineffective and in poor taste.

Another avenue open to public opinion is our Congress. Congressional leaders have shown that they recognize the importance of physical outdoor activities such as hiking. In spite of the current administration, Congress has enough clout to protect our wild places. And like the Forest Service, Congress pays attention to personal letters (rather than photocopied notes or generic mass emails) regarding funding for trails and designation of wild areas. Let them know what areas need trails, for public access

Forested trail on the Pass Creek–Cady Pass loop

onto public lands, and what areas need wilderness designation.

Write a letter today: *Ask for the Wild Sky region to be designated as wilderness.* You have an opportunity to influence the geography of hiking in Washington State. By writing to the Forest Service and to Congress, you can become part of a legacy of trails, giving future generations the opportunity to experience the wealth of our wild areas in the beauty of early springtime blossoms, a sunny summer forest, the golden leaves of autumn, or a frozen mountain creek.

Ira Spring
April 2003

HEALTHY TRAILS MAKE HEALTHY PEOPLE

This book does more than describe paths to beautiful destinations in the Cascade Mountains. It also offers paths to good health.

Physical activities such as walking and hiking improve physical and mental health, reduce risk of major diseases including heart disease, high blood pressure, diabetes, obesity, and colon cancer, and increase longevity. The U.S. Surgeon General recommends that people of all ages include a moderate amount of physical activity in their daily routine. On at least five days of the week, people should expend at least 150–200 additional calories daily by performing moderate-intensity activities such as walking.

But during the twentieth century, Americans became less and less physically active. Currently, 30 percent of adults are completely sedentary during their leisure time, and another 30 percent to 40 percent are minimally active. Preventable diseases, such as obesity and diabetes, are increasing dramatically. In the last decade, there was a 61 percent increase in the percentage of Americans who are obese (12 percent to 19.8 percent), and a 49 percent increase in the percentage of Americans who have diabetes (4.9 percent to 7.3 percent). In 1999, over 13 percent of children age six to eleven were overweight.

But as we encourage Americans to be more physically active, we also should provide them with ample opportunities to be active. We need communities with "physical activity–friendly" environments. Part of the solution is building and maintaining the marvelous recreational trails described in this book.

I hope the hikes in this book become part of your pursuit of an active lifestyle. While most of these hikes exceed a moderate amount of activity, the good news is you gain additional health benefits through greater amounts of activity. When you aren't in the backcountry, integrate physical activity into your daily life. Find enjoyable ways to be active, from biking to work, walking a golf course, and playing sports to gardening, kayaking, and dancing—there are many, many pleasant ways to become fit and healthy.

David M. Buchner, MD, MPH
Chief, Physical Activity and Health Branch
Division of Nutrition and Physical Activity
U.S. Centers for Disease Control and Prevention

Town of Index from the top of Index Town Wall

INDEX, WASHINGTON: GATEWAY TO THE WILD SKY WILDERNESS

Index residents are fortunate to live in a spectacular natural setting. From any street in our town you can see magnificent mountain peaks flanked by hillsides covered in unbroken forests stretching for miles. But even though most all the land visible from Index and up the North Fork valley is publicly owned, very little of it has any formal, legislative protection.

Most of us would like to see these lands stay wild and don't want to see roads built and forests cut down. Congressionally designated Wilderness is the strongest, most durable protection possible for public lands, and it still allows for a broad range of recreational activities. That's why I support Senator Patty Murray and Congressman Rick Larsen's efforts to protect these places.

As much as I like living here, it's just as enjoyable to share this natural splendor with visitors who come from near and far to experience a little of what we have. I enjoy pointing out Mount Index, Mount Persis, and Gunn Peak and seeing the thrill in visitors' eyes as they look through the transparent blue-green waters of the North Fork and maybe catch a glimpse of a salmon or steelhead migrating home.

I'm proud of the pristine environment surrounding Index, and I want to make sure that residents and visitors can continue to enjoy this beauty for many generations to come.

Years ago, Index was a logging town and the old-growth forests on many of the accessible lower mountain slopes were cut. Since then, almost all that area has grown back, and will once again be old growth in little more than the span of a human lifetime. The forests of the North Fork tend to grow on steep slopes and are more valuable for watershed protection and flood control and scenery than as commercial timber.

We are proud of our logging heritage, but we look forward to a new way of life in the 21st century. The logging jobs of yesteryear are being replaced by a more sustainable economy tied to outdoor recreation.

As more people come to Index and the North Fork valley, they bring with them a new economy when they stop in the stores, eat in the restaurants, and hire locals as fishing and river guides. While this new economy may not have quite the drama of the highball logging days, it is growing steadily. The real glory days of logging here lasted only a few decades. The new recreation and amenity based economy has the potential to go on forever. Protecting much of the North Fork valley as Wilderness will help insure that it does.

Recently a friend of mine returned from Europe. As he looked out the window as the plane descended toward Seattle, the clouds began to part and reveal the landscape below. He told me his heart skipped a few beats as he realized he was looking down at the North Fork valley.

"It was incredible," my friend said. "Unbroken forests covered everything except the river and mountaintops. There it all was, and it was then that I realized that there is nothing remotely like it in all of Europe. It was so beautiful, it just about brought tears to my eyes to know I was back home."

And he was right. Here in Index we are fortunate to live in a spectacular part of one of the most beautiful areas in the world. I invite you to visit Index and the North Fork valley and enjoy these lovely places, and I invite you to join me in efforts to support the Wild Sky Wilderness.

Kem Hunter
Mayor of Index

Reprinted courtesy of the Seattle Post-Intelligencer, *June 13, 2002.*

Opposite: *Bridal Veil Falls*

INTRODUCTION

The Wild Sky Country and Beyond

Few other cities in the world the size of Seattle are as fortunate in having so much wild country literally within sight. On a clear day, the Olympics to the west and the Cascades to the east, from Mount Baker down to Mount Rainier, present an unparalleled, unforgettable view. Looking directly east, especially from north Seattle up to around Everett, a good part of what one sees is the Wild Skykomish, or "Wild Sky" country. This is a region of lonely summits, quiet lakes and meadows, and deep, dark forests, centered on the valleys of the North and South Forks of the Skykomish River, their tributaries, and surrounding mountains. The interesting, diverse landscapes of the Skykomish country as well as the areas along Highway 2 east of Stevens Pass to Leavenworth, and how best to reach and enjoy them, are the subject of this book.

Real wild country is abundant near Highway 2—the Stevens Pass Highway, the "other" way across the Cascades—much more so than in the heavily logged landscapes of Interstate 90, the "main street of the Northwest," and the Snoqualmie Pass country. The Highway 2 corridor and environs on the west side of the mountains—the Wild Sky country—have emerged as a major conservation priority. In February 2003, Senator Patty Murray and Congressman Rick Larsen introduced bills to designate 106,000 acres north of Highway 2 as the "Wild Sky Wilderness." Congresswoman Jennifer Dunn is also a cosponsor. The boundaries of this proposed wilderness have been drawn specifically to include large areas of biologically rich low-elevation lands and salmon streams. If successful, it will break the mold that has thus far kept most previously designated wilderness areas confined to less productive, higher-elevation lands—"rocks and ice." Conservationists hope that the Wild Sky Wilderness will set a precedent in protecting the rich lowlands that are the real heart of this ecosystem.

The heart of the Wild Sky proposal is the North Fork Skykomish valley. From the attractive mountain town of Index, the valley of the North Fork stretches north and east to the crest of the Cascades. From an elevation of only 600 feet at Index, the terrain rises to over 7000 feet atop Columbia and Kyes Peaks. In between are some of the most extensive natural forests in the Cascades, both old growth and second growth, and some of the best salmon waters near Puget Sound. The North Fork waters have a pleasing blue-green transparency and are home to healthy populations of fish.

West of the North Fork valley, the Ragged Ridge country comprises the western unit of the Wild Sky. From Arsenic Meadows to Northstar Mountain, this is some of the loneliest terrain in the Cascades, although much of it is within sight of downtown Seattle. No formal trails exist here—just the rough path to Lake Isabel (Hike 5). This is wilderness in the truest sense, a place where few people go, a great big blank spot on the map.

East of the lower North Fork is the "Sky Peaks" unit of the Wild Sky proposal (also known as the Eagle Rock roadless area). Spectacular peaks

North Fork Skykomish valley, centerpiece of the Wild Sky country, from Scott Peak; Mounts Index and Persis behind Photo by John Roper

such as Gunn, Merchant, and Baring dominate its southern end, while farther north, the valleys of upper Trout and Howard Creeks hold extensive virgin forests. Seldom-visited lakes lie at the heads of many valleys. The central and northern reaches of the Sky Peaks/Eagle Rock area are a mysterious, little-known region. Dense forests and rough terrain can make for slow traveling. Some places probably go for years without seeing a human. If there is a corner of the Cascades where a grizzly bear could call home, this is surely it.

As one moves farther up the North Fork, the mountains become gentler. Long ridges are topped by extensive flower meadows, and large areas of old growth forest cloak many of the slopes and valley bottoms. This is friendly, inviting country, slightly drier than areas farther west. There are a number of popular trails here, such as the North Fork trail (Hike 13) and West Cady Ridge trail (Hike 11). Certain areas lend themselves to off-trail wandering through open forests and meadows. The valleys of the upper North Fork Skykomish and West Cady Creek support particularly extensive areas of unbroken ancient forest.

Congressionally designated wilderness is the strongest, most durable protection possible for public land. If successful, the Wild Sky Wilderness will protect about 60,000 acres of middle- and upper-elevation old growth forests and 14,000 acres of low-elevation (below 3000 feet) old growth. Around

Old growth Douglas firs, North Fork Skykomish valley
Photo by Kevin Geraghty

25 miles of salmon and steelhead spawning streams are included—far more than in any other wilderness area in the Cascades. About 6000 acres of the naturally regenerated second growth forests surrounding the spawning grounds would also be preserved.

Probably any one of these areas would have been designated as a national park if it had been located next to any other major U.S. city, but there are so many spectacular places in this region that they have been taken for granted. Even after a century of logging, the Skykomish still has extensive ancient forests and maturing second growth forests in the lower valleys. By protecting what is left and restoring damaged areas, we can help ensure the survival of salmon and other wildlife. The Wild Sky proposal is a historic opportunity to keep the Skykomish wild. We invite you to explore the Wild Sky and other areas along Highway 2 described in this book and to join the efforts to enact the Wild Sky Wilderness.

About This Book

This is the first hiking guide to day hikes reached from Highway 2, also commonly referred to as the Stevens Pass Highway. Those who want information about longer backpack hikes or places beyond the coverage of this book should refer to two other volumes from The Mountaineers Books, *100 Hikes in Washington's Glacier Peak Region: The North Cascades* (for areas north of Highway 2) and *100 Hikes in Washington's Alpine Lakes* (for areas south of Highway 2). Each of these covers a larger portion of the Cascades than this book, though in somewhat less detail.

This book is separated into two sections: the Highway 2 Mileposts section and the Hikes section. The Mileposts section details features, views, and short walks along Highway 2 or on side roads that head off the highway, cued to the green milepost numbers found along the highway that begin at 0 in Everett. The section ends at milepost 150, near Waterville, east of the mountains.

In the Hikes section, every official trail in the Skykomish region west of Stevens Pass is described, short ones and long ones, as well as a number of unofficial routes and old roads that are returning to nature and once again offer pleasant hiking. Trees grow quickly in the Cascades, and many places that suffered earlier logging are once again worth visiting. A number of trails and hiking possibilities east of Stevens Pass are also described, including the Tumwater Canyon, Leavenworth, and Icicle Valley areas, with the emphasis again on day hiking. East-side trails where the main attractions are beyond day-hike range have been omitted. For these, see the two volumes listed above.

Hikes are numbered 1 through 55, west to east, according to where one turns off of Highway 2. At the end of this section you'll find ten "bonus" hikes—very short walks featuring a quick escape to nature that anyone can find time to enjoy. Each hike has a description highlighting the major attractions. The descriptions are preceded by the trip's vital statistics: round trip in miles, elevation gain, high point. An estimate of the round-trip hiking time is also given. This will naturally vary from hiker to hiker. A motivated hiker in good shape should in most cases have no trouble moving much faster than the stated time; a dedicated couch potato emerging after a winter spent indoors should probably allow somewhat more time. The "hikable," or snowfree, season for each trail is listed. This will vary from year to year depending on recent weather and the previous winter's snowfall. These, too, are only estimates. An estimate of the use level for each hike is also given. Generally, those listed as having light or moderate use have tended not to attract crowds, sometimes because of strenuous climbs or difficult access. This can change over time, and there is no guarantee that there won't be a crowd the day you decide to go. Those listed as receiving heavy or very heavy use will normally attract multiple parties on any nice weekend day. Solitude may be hard to find at these places except during the proverbial rainy Tuesday in February, and perhaps not even then.

Outdoor Practicalities

This book doesn't tell you how to hike or what kind of shoes to wear; there are many books available on the subject of hiking, so we won't cover that here. However, there are a number of practical issues that bear repeating anytime one decides to step into the great outdoors.

The Ten Essentials

No hiking guide would be complete without listing the Ten Essentials. This list has evolved from the original ten items found over years of usage by The Mountaineers to be most effective for protection and safety while enjoying the outdoors. The new approach lists items by "system." Be sure to bring these with you on all hikes; there is no guarantee that even a short walk won't find you stranded and in need of one or more of these emergency systems.

1. Navigation (map and compass)
2. Sun protection (sunglasses and sunscreen)
3. Insulation (extra clothing)
4. Illumination (headlamp or flashlight)
5. First-aid supplies
6. Fire (firestarter and matches/lighter)
7. Repair kit and tools (including knife)
8. Nutrition (extra food)
9. Hydration (extra water)
10. Emergency shelter

Safety

Unplanned nights out can happen. The items listed above can make the difference between an inconvenience and an ordeal. Most authorities recommend that a hiker, particularly a solo hiker, leave word with friends or family as to their destination and expected return time. Cell phones have led to an epidemic of search-and-rescue calls from those who are merely cold, wet, and tired rather than truly life-threatened. Don't depend on a cell phone to work in mountainous terrain. They normally function only within line-of-sight of towns or major highways. Portable satellite phones ("Globalstar" and "Iridium" are the two available systems) have come way down in price in recent years and will work in any open area, but are no substitute for planning and common sense.

Maps

The maps in this book are intended to give only a general sense of the hikes and terrain they represent. Additional maps are essential for navigating both roads and trails.

Once off Highway 2, the U.S. Forest Service uses a numerical system to identify roads. Main roads are given two numbers (for instance, 64); secondary roads off main roads include the numbers of the main road plus two more (for instance, 6405). Spur roads from these secondary roads add another three numbers to the four-digit identification, and are usually identified on road signs with just three numbers.

You'll need to take two types of maps with you: one for driving and one (or more) for hiking. National forest recreation maps are a good choice for exploring roads off Highway 2. Green Trails series maps and USGS 7½-minute maps are best for hiking. Green Trails maps show all maintained trails and generally cover larger areas than USGS maps. Their topography is not nearly as detailed as USGS maps, though, and if you plan on doing any off-trail exploring or just want the best possible maps, USGS quadrangles are the only choice. Individual sheets tend to be expensive, but a good alternative is to purchase the entire set on CD-ROM (one brand is called "Topo!") and print off disposable copies as needed. Ranger stations, map shops, and sporting goods stores carry a variety of maps. Whichever ones you choose, be sure they cover the area you plan to explore.

Insects

Insects are seldom more than an annoyance in the Cascades. However, hornets and yellow jackets are very defensive about their nests, since grubs are a favorite food of bears, which will endure hundreds of stings for such a meal. Usually it is the second or third person in line who gets hit. Running makes sense, and intruders will seldom be pursued more than 30 or

Hiker with pack goats, looking north from Scorpion Mountain (Hike 21) to Rapid River valley Photo by Rick McGuire

40 feet. Warm days in late summer or early fall are when yellow jackets are most defensive. Suctioning devices can pull out some venom if used immediately after a sting.

Few experiences are as unpleasant as finding an embedded tick during an after-hike shower. Ticks are common on the east side in spring, and it pays to wear light-colored clothing and check oneself frequently. The west side has few ticks, and they tend to be larger and easier to spot than those on the east side. But their scarcity means that few people check for them—a mistake that those who have been bitten once take care not to repeat. None of the folk remedies that purport to make ticks pull out of the skin actually work, and there is no way to deal with them other than to perform minor but still gruesome surgery, digging them out with a sharp, and hopefully sterile, implement. You'll find out who your real friends are when you ask for help in dealing with a tick.

Bears

In the unlikely event of a confrontation with a bear, do not run away. Bears can run fast (faster than most dogs) and will sometimes reflexively chase someone who flees. Don't make any sudden moves and slowly move away. Talk softly, look away, and act as though you're willing to ignore the bear if it ignores you. Most bears are well mannered, and none are looking for fights with people. They just want to get on with their lives. The only problem bears are those that have been habituated to associate people with food. Keep a clean camp so as not to encourage bad habits, which too often result in the bear getting shot.

Dogs

The subject of dogs in the outdoors has been debated at great length. Few people nowadays have the time to properly train a dog, and dogs can annoy other hikers and chase away wildlife. But they are fun companions, they are available when you are, and exercise does them a world of good, just as it does for people. Some writers advocate taking leashed dogs on hiking trails. But, realistically, who wants to keep their dog on a leash in the great outdoors? Most of the fun of taking dogs out is letting them run free, to just be a dog. This doesn't work well on trails but does work in many less-traveled parts of the Cascades.

If you must take your dog hiking, especially avoid summertime berry fields, where the chances are high of meeting up with bears. It's unfortunate, but bears and dogs just do not get along, and bears see even gentle dogs as a threat. A dog will invariably run from a bear straight back to its owner, and then keep running, leaving the owner to deal with the bear. Mother bears with cubs have a special dislike for dogs. The authors recommend against taking dogs on the trails described herein. Instead, use a map and seek out more obscure places better suited for letting a dog run free. Foothill forests have far fewer bears than summer meadows. Dogs are not judgmental and will love you just as much even if the place you take them is not one of the scenic climaxes of the Cascades. You might even find a new favorite spot.

Off-trail Hiking

If some trails seem too crowded, consider giving off-trail hiking a try. Cross-country hiking offers the mental exercise of routefinding in addition to physical exercise using all parts of the body. The wetter parts of the Cascades are justly famous for brush, but there are also many places where the forest canopy shades out undergrowth, making for easy walking. The western front range gets the most rain and has the most brush. Terrain grows noticeably less brushy as one moves east, even when still west of the crest. Drier east-side and alpine areas are often quite open, as are most forests above 4000 feet. Even in lower west-side forests, it's often surprisingly easy to get around by choosing routes along well-drained slopes and ridges and avoiding gullies. Always hike under the heaviest timber possible. Start out with modest goals, and keep in mind that 1 mile off trail may take as much time as 5 miles or more on a trail.

Topping out on Ragged Ridge, Mount Baring in the distance
Photo by Kevin Geraghty

A 7½-minute USGS quadrangle map and the ability to use it are essential. Compasses, altimeters, GPS receivers, and even aerial photos, though seldom really necessary, can all be deployed to demystify a place. You'll never find a crowd off trail, and the extra dimensions of finding untraveled places and thinking about your route instead of just following a path can be very satisfying.

Protect Your Trails

Whether on or off trail, no matter where you go in the Cascades, think about how you can help protect the place. Pack out as much as you can of any trash you find, including flagging. Treat the land as if you own it—because you do. The public lands of the Cascades are utterly dependent on their watchful public owners to protect them. It would be nice if we could all sit back and entrust that job to those who are paid to do it, but those people are few in number. Help them do their job by reporting any suspicious or clearly illegal activities, such as tree poaching, wild shooting, or garbage dumping.

The Cascades have much to give, but trails need all the help they can get. While shrinking Forest Service budgets have meant fewer destructive schemes in recent years, they've also meant less maintenance for trails. Volunteers have helped fill the gap on many trails. Consider lending a hand by joining a trail work party. Washington Trails Association (1305 Fourth Avenue, Room 512, Seattle, WA 98101; *www.wta.org*) offers many such opportunities. Get involved, give something back, and do what you can to ensure that others can enjoy the same places we've been so fortunate to have. Most of all, have fun.

A Note about Safety

Safety is an important concern in all outdoor activities. No guidebook can alert you to every hazard or anticipate the limitations of every reader. Therefore, the descriptions of roads, trails, routes, and natural features in this book are not representations that a particular place or excursion will be safe for your party. When you follow any of the routes described in this book, you assume responsibility for your own safety. Under normal conditions, such excursions require the usual attention to traffic, road and trail conditions, weather, terrain, the capabilities of your party, and other factors. Keeping informed on current conditions and exercising common sense are the keys to a safe, enjoyable outing.

The Mountaineers Books

Opposite: *Snow-clad Mount Index from the Stevens Pass Highway*

U.S. HIGHWAY 2

Stevens Pass National Scenic Byway

U.S. Highway 2 traverses the northern tier of states from Everett, Washington, to the Straits of Mackinac, in northern Michigan. People in western Washington know it as the Stevens Pass Highway, the "other" way across the Cascades. The section of Highway 2 covered in this volume, from Everett (mile 0) east to Wenatchee and Waterville (mile 150), passes through some of the most scenic mountain country of any highway in the U.S. But with few pull-offs, the best views can be had only at 60 miles an hour—unless you head off the highway to enjoy the area at a more leisurely pace.

This is the first volume in the *100 Hikes* series from The Mountaineers Books to cover mountain roads as well as trails. Most of the lower valleys have roads in them, many of which need to be closed and converted to trail, and some of which are closing themselves through time and neglect. In this section, you'll find highlights of some of the views and features to be seen from Highway 2 and most of the major side roads leading into the mountains from it, as well as descriptions of some pleasant walking possibilities which, due to their shortness or unofficial status, don't really qualify as "hikes." Distances are keyed to the green mileposts along the highway that start at mile 0 in Everett. Distances along side roads are listed in miles from Highway 2. Few of these roads have visible mileposts, and every car odometer is slightly different, so the figures are approximate. The hikes described in this book, and their numbers, are noted along the way.

Highway 2 is a beautiful drive—just not on rainy nights. The spectacle of Mount Index rising 5500 feet from the Skykomish is unmatched. The Forest Service has recognized the corridor's significance by designating the segment within the national forests as a "Scenic Byway," meaning that views from the highway should be protected if possible. The Stevens Pass Greenway is a volunteer group that has taken up the goal of protecting the corridor. Much of the "scenery" is relatively secure in the national forests, but certainly not all of it. Visitor facilities, though still few, will grow over time and provide more opportunities to enjoy the attractions along the way. Be aware that heavy traffic going east on Friday nights and Saturdays, and west on Sundays, can really slow things down. A fair amount of housing has been thrown up in Sultan and Gold Bar in recent years without any highway improvements to handle the resulting commuter traffic. This has inevitably led to traffic problems, especially heading east on rainy winter evenings.

The Stevens Pass Highway is scenic but dangerous, and should be driven cautiously and defensively. The thinking of the highway department has always been against making moderate, incremental safety improvements all along the road, which could make for a safer highway sitting more lightly on the land. Instead, some segments are vastly overbuilt, while other infamous death traps, such as the Anderson Creek bridge, west of Index, haven't changed since the first Model T rolled across. Perverse budgetary incentives drive the decisions—it's easier to secure funds

North Fork Skykomish valley from San Juan Mountain

to completely rebuild short parts of the road than to gradually improve all of it. Many mountain highways in Europe and California have been built to be safe without overbuilding. Highways don't necessarily have to be ugly, but the ingrained "all-or-nothing" approach to roads in this state too often makes them so.

Whatever faults it may have, no one can dispute that Highway 2 is the way to get to some of the most interesting and scenic mountain country to be found anywhere. From Everett in the west to Wenatchee and Waterville in the east, it's one dramatic landscape after another. No matter how many times you may drive it, you will never be bored.

Highway 2 Mileposts

Beginning on Highway 2

Mile 0: Everett. Most mountain watchers agree that Everett has the best views of the Cascades of any city on Puget Sound. The valleys line up to allow views far up the Sultan, Skykomish, and Snoqualmie drainages, without blocking foothills. Glacier Peak can be seen, Pilchuck is close enough to reveal individual trees, Three Fingers dominates the northeast, and the eternally white mass of Mount Baker stands to the north. Situated on a north-jutting peninsula between Port Gardner bay and the Snohomish River and estuary, it's such a beautiful locale that nothing seems able to ruin it.

Mile 2–4: Snohomish valley. Once a vast wetland, most of it was diked and drained for farmland, but some areas remain natural and others have been "re-reclaimed" by breaching dikes and letting the water back in. On the east side of the valley the highway turns south and passes above a large area of bottomland spruce forest managed by the Washington Department of Fish and Wildlife.

Mile 5: Junction with State Highway 9, views ahead to the leaning tower of Mount Baring.

Mile 6: Pilchuck River. The Snohomish–Lake Stevens Centennial Trail is crossed.

Mile 8: Exit to the city of Snohomish, with its attractively original main street along the Snohomish River, fine old buildings and houses, antique shops, and restaurants.

Mile 9–12: Views of Mount Rainier, pastures, and hybrid cottonwood plantations.

Mile 14: Evergreen State Fairgrounds. The fair opens the last week of August. Turnoff for Highway 522 to Woodinville and Seattle.

Mile 14–15: Monroe. The Cascades are visibly closer. Just south of here, the Skykomish and Snoqualmie Rivers unite to form the Snohomish River, which flows into Puget Sound at Everett. Strip malls and shopping centers have erased all charm along the highway, but Main Street, a few blocks south, has a nice small-town feel. At the east end of town, Buck Island Park protects an extensive stretch of river-bottom maple and cottonwood forest along the Skykomish. To find it, turn south off Highway 2 to Main Street at the easternmost traffic light. Cross the railroad tracks, then make an immediate hard left onto Railroad Street. Follow it east and south a couple of blocks to where it ends at Simons Street; turn left and reach the park entrance shortly. Several short trails provide walking opportunities. One of the best times to visit is in early

April when the cottonwoods just begin leafing out, their bursting buds scenting the air.

Mile 19–22: Views ahead: Mount Stickney to the left, upper Wallace valley in the U-shaped slot that appears to be straight ahead, and Gunn and Merchant Peaks farther to the right.

Mile 22: Sultan. The confluence of the Sultan and Skykomish Rivers at the west end of the town was once an Indian village site, and is still a popular fishing spot. In early fall of odd-numbered years, this can be a good place to see pink salmon. Park at the Wildlife Department fishing access just north of the highway and walk upstream along the Sultan River. It's also possible to go back west a quarter of a mile to a traffic light, and turn north for another quarter of a mile or less, to reach a city park to access the Sultan River farther upstream. In years with good returns it's easy to see—and smell—quite a few fish here. Try not to crowd any wildlife that may need a meal.

Mile 22 Side Trip: Sultan Basin

Thirteen miles north of Highway 2, at the western foot of the Cascade front range, is the rugged, rainy, little-known Sultan Basin, where such major peaks as Big Four, Vesper, and Del Campo stand high above headwater valleys. The basin was almost untouched until 1960, when its lower reaches were flooded to store water for Everett. Three decades of heavy logging followed, believed by many to have led to abnormally high asbestos levels in the water. The Sultan dam, and one supplying water to Seattle on the Tolt River, is the only major impoundment in the Snohomish watershed. The Sultan water system provides considerably more water than the combined output of Seattle's Tolt and Cedar watersheds. The City of Everett controls access, and the basin is currently open for day use, though that could change. Only two foot trails are officially maintained, but a number of roads in various states of decay offer exploring possibilities up remote tributary valleys.

Mile 0: The Sultan Basin road turns north from Highway 2 just before the top of a hill on the east side of the town of Sultan. It may be difficult to turn on to from the eastbound lanes; if so, go farther up the highway, turn around, and enter it westbound. The road passes several dreary subdivisions before climbing a long hill through former farm fields with expansive views of the Cascades and the valley below.

Mile 2: A left turn on 116th Street leads to a City of Everett gate, which may be open at times. Park here, or continue on if it's open (pay attention to when it may be locked; there should be a sign) to another gate above the Snohomish County Public Utility District (PUD) powerhouse on the Sultan River. It's possible to walk ever-changing logging roads north from here to the Horseshoe Bend area of the Sultan River canyon.

Mile 3: The paved Kellogg Lake road leads east and south through private timberlands to rejoin Highway 2 at Startup.

Mile 4–11: The Sultan Basin road passes a number of side roads and clearings that have attracted an unsavory clientele. Dumping and "target" shooting have given the place a bad reputation. Law enforcement has tried to cover the area more effectively, but the sheriff's deputies who cover eastern Snohomish County are few in number and have a lot of country to watch. The state Department of Natural Resources has responded by gating and closing off problem areas. A non-profit private group, Friends of the Trail, which has done much to turn around a similar situation in the Middle Fork Snoqualmie valley near North Bend, has organized cleanup efforts, and progress is being made. It's okay to park at gates and walk or mountain bike in on closed roads.

Mile 5.4: The gated Marsh Creek road is the entry point to miles of logging roads at the foot of and on top of Blue Mountain. Depending on recent logging activity, some of these have good views, and the views from the 3100-foot summit of Blue Mountain are spectacular. Newer and older roads can also be followed toward the Sultan River canyon.

Steelhead fishing in the Skykomish River near Goldbar

Mile 13.6: Olney Pass, and a three-way road junction. The actual Sultan Basin and City of Everett watershed are entered here. The road may be gated. Opening times are posted, and visitors are required to sign in. The gated left fork leads down to the Culmback Dam on the Sultan, which holds back the Spada Reservoir. The center fork accesses the Sultan Basin, which is open for day use only except for Greider and Boulder Lakes (Hikes 1 and 2), where camping is permitted mid-June to mid-October.

The right fork offers an interesting trip into the Kromona Mine Basin beneath the north side of Mount Stickney. From Olney Pass, go hard right and follow the gated road about 4 nearly level miles to the southeast. Some good views can be had from the road of The Shards, a collection of steep rock peaklets above the North Fork of the South Fork Sultan, an awkwardly named but mysterious and wild valley. The road enters the Middle Fork of the South Fork valley and circles to the long-abandoned Kromona Mine works (no bridge) in a partly treeless basin. Mount Stickney rises to the southwest and Prospect Peak to the east.

Mile 15: The road descends to cross the South Fork Sultan, then contours northwest and northeast above the Spada Reservoir.

Mile 20.7: Greider Lake trailhead (Hike 1). The road continues 1.2 miles to the Boulder Lake trailhead (Hike 2). It may be drivable farther but soon becomes too rough for vehicles. It can be walked another mile or more into steep, brushy Elk Basin.

At low water it's also possible to hike an old mining road into the spectacular North Fork Sultan valley (Hike 3).

Back on Highway 2

Mile 25: Small rest area along the highway beside the Wallace River. Poor views, but salmon can sometimes be seen in the Wallace.

Mile 25–27: Startup. The unincorporated "town" of Startup is passed, with its many churches both abandoned and new. Cross the Wallace River on an old cantilever bridge; the mountain views grow dramatically.

Mile 28: Gold Bar. Turnoff for Wallace Falls (Hike 4) is at the west end of town; follow signs.

The town of Gold Bar is in a spectacular spot where the Skykomish River leaves the mountains, its valley broadening dramatically. The "braided channel" reach of the river starts here and extends down to Sultan. This is the site of the greatest extent of salmon-spawning grounds in the entire Snohomish watershed, critical habitat for Chinook, pink, coho, and chum salmon.

The Cascade front range forms an impressive half-ring of mountains around Gold Bar. Directly north, the long west ridge of Mount Stickney is capped by a 5367-foot summit, with over 5000 feet of relief between Gold Bar and the top. Immediately below it is the white cascade of Wallace Falls. To the northeast, above and behind Wallace Falls to the right, is a puzzlingly unnamed but very prominent mountain with three round wooded summits, 4865 feet at its highest point. (One of its unofficial names is "Cabin Ridge.") Lake Isabel (Hike 5) sits in the next notch to the east, and to the right of it is the "Arsenic Meadows" area, the southern end of the little-known Ragged Ridge country. Continuing right, the steep, sharp peaks of Gunn, Merchant, and Baring form a truly spectacular vista to the east. Farther right, Mount Index is largely hidden behind the high ridge of Mount Persis. Continuing clockwise, the view is completed by Haystack Mountain directly south. Most of it has been and continues to be logged intensively, but about 1500 acres of old growth forest remain on national forest land on the top, visible from here. This 1500-acre forest may be the closest old growth forest of such size to Puget Sound. It is an important refuge for marbled murrelets, spotted owls, and other wildlife, including ravens, who fly in from far and wide to use it as a roosting site amid the otherwise heavily logged Cascade foothills.

Mile 30: Reiter Road turnoff (north). Access to old roads and the trail to Lake Isabel (Hike 5). The area along Reiter Road unfortunately is a major ORV playground. Reiter Road follows the north side of the Skykomish to the town of Index, though there are few views unless there has been recent logging. About 3 miles from the highway a side road accesses Deer Creek Flat. No trails, but old logging grades can be followed to some viewpoints above the Index Town Wall and looking up the North Fork Skykomish valley. Expect ORVs on weekends.

Just across the Skykomish River bridge on the east side is the Big Eddy River access and the beginning of the Skykomish State Scenic River designation. Sandbars for kids, swimming in summer (yes, it is possible), and a popular raft and boat launch and pullout.

Mile 32: The highway rounds a bend and comes face to face with the northwest walls of Mount Index, one of the most spectacular mountain views in the state. Unfortunately, there is no easy pull-off. There is a safe but small pull-off in the middle of the big bend on the south side of the road. There is also a gravel area on the north side of the highway just before the curve, and it is possible to park here and hike along a riverside path upstream to views of Index. "Boulder Drop," a popular kayak run, is just above here. The gravel area is best approached from the westbound lane.

Mile 33: Just after crossing "No Name Creek" (sign is often missing), Forest Service road 62 goes right and climbs through private land into the Proctor Creek valley. At about 3 miles, a left fork (road 6220) leads to a scenic basin below Mount Persis. The other fork (road 62) leads to a gate

Mount Baring from a viewpoint above Goldbar

at Dry Creek Pass and can be bicycled beyond the gate into the Tolt valley and the John Hancock Snoqualmie Tree Farm. Old roads lead high up the not-so-steep south side of Mount Index, and to over 150 square miles of little-known mountains, rivers, and lakes. To the west, a maze of logging roads can be followed to Haystack Mountain, where one of the closest old growth forests to Puget Sound can be found on several square miles of national forest land. Vehicular access to the tree farm is possible by fee permit on weekends from North Bend and Snoqualmie only, with the Dry Creek gate always closed. Vehicle permits can be bought at some sporting goods stores. For the most part, this is very lonely country.

Mile 34: An old commercial campground here between the highway and the river has been purchased by the state, though not developed. It's possible to park outside the gate and walk down to the river and views of Mount Baring. The forested slopes immediately above the river to the north are protected in a state park.

Mile 35: The Mount Index county road goes right here, and at 0.3 mile is the Lake Serene trailhead (Hike 6). The county road ends at 1.6 miles, within view of the spectacular chute of Sunset Falls, one of the scenic wonders of the Skykomish. Unfortunately, there is no public access to the falls.

The highway crosses an old and dangerous bridge to the north side of the river. It's possible, though risky, to pull off and park in a gravel area on the north side of the highway west of the bridge. A sidewalk can be walked out to views at midspan, but heavy traffic and powerlines spoil the vista. Far better, safer, and quieter views can be had from the town of Index a mile north. The North Fork Skykomish road, also known as the Index–Galena road, leads north shortly past the bridge.

MILE 35 SIDE TRIP: NORTH FORK SKYKOMISH

In a mountain range full of scenic valleys, the North Fork Skykomish stands out as an especially interesting place. Most of it is south or west facing, giving it a particular richness and warmth. Uniquely among Cascade rivers, anadromous fish can ascend its upper reaches to within 5 miles of the crest. Much old growth forest survives in the upper valley and in tributary valleys. The lower 10 miles were railroad logged early in the twentieth century but have now grown back with beautiful, diverse, naturally regenerated second growth forests, well on their way to becoming old growth. The outstanding forest and fish values have made the North Fork the centerpiece of the Wild Sky Wilderness proposal, which was designed to include most of the valley to keep it the way it is. Numerous trails offer ways into the wilderness, from short walks to long hikes.

Mile 0: The North Fork Skykomish road, also known as the Index–Galena road for the first 10 miles, turns north from Highway 2 at the Mount Index Café. A 30-mile loop can be driven up the North Fork Sky, over Jack Pass, and down the Beckler valley to rejoin Highway 2.

Mile 1: Index. Possibly the most attractive mountain town in Washington, with views no one could ever tire of. A graceful steel arch and cable bridge crosses the North Fork, proof that roads and bridges can be beautiful as well as utilitarian. Immediately after the bridge, parking is available on both sides of the street, with the town park to the left and a store to the right. Structural problems closed the historic Bush House Hotel and restaurant as of early 2003. The Pickett Museum has a number of interesting items and is open weekends from noon to 3:00 P.M., from Memorial Day to the end of September.

Index is by far the best place from which to see the views that fly by on the highway. The most prominent mountain to the south is of course Mount Index, with a high ridge connecting west to Mount Persis, making them two parts of the same massif. To the west is the Index Town Wall, pieces of which have been quarried and shipped far and wide. Peregrine falcons sometimes nest on the cliffs. To the northeast are the high rocky cliffs of Jumpoff Ridge, which runs up into the Gunn Peak massif, with the high wooded valley of Lewis Creek in front.

The river can be accessed behind the museum. It's a good picnic spot and a place to look for pink salmon in the early fall of odd-numbered years.

Mile 2.4–2.6: "Hall of Mosses." Many large, moss-draped bigleaf maples line the road here, and the light-green moss is especially striking on sunny winter and early spring days.

Mile 2.6: Lewis Creek road. A large parking area is here. The gated

Bush House Hotel, built in 1898 Photo by Conway Leovy

Lewis Creek road offers good walking when higher areas are snow covered and good mountain biking all year. The road can be followed up to Heybrook Ridge and lookout, reached also by trail from the south (Hike 16).

Mile 4.2: An especially nice stretch of natural second growth forest can be seen along the road here. The lower 10 miles of the North Fork valley were railroad logged in the 1920s and have now grown back with beautiful, naturally regenerated forest like that seen here.

Mile 6.2: Trout Creek. Old roads can be walked here. See Hike 7.

Mile 9.1: North Fork bridge to the left. A concrete bridge crosses the North Fork with good views downstream to Mount Index and Mount Persis. Across it, roads lead straight to Mineral Butte (Hike 8) and right to Silver Creek (Hike 9). The Silver Creek gorge makes a nice short walk for those not afraid of heights.

Mile 10.2: North Fork bridge. The road crosses to the north side of the valley and enters forest that has never been logged. During winter the road is normally plowed to a large gravel area just across the bridge and closed beyond. It's often possible to walk along snowmobile tracks, or the road itself, a mile upstream to Troublesome Creek for a short winter hike.

Mile 11.2: Troublesome Creek. A campground and short loop trail along Troublesome Creek to a rock gorge, one of the best short walks in the Skykomish country. See Bonus Walk 1.

Mile 11.2–13: The road cuts through impressive ancient forest, some of it 700 years old. Many tall Douglas fir trees, some pushing 6 feet in diameter, can be seen from the road.

Mile 13.2: San Juan Campground. About ten sites are located here between the road and river. The steep northern slopes of Bear Mountain rise abruptly just across the river.

Mile 13.7: Garland Mineral Springs bypass. Garland Mineral Springs (the water is only lukewarm, not hot) was once the site of a resort, of which nothing remains but "No Trespassing" signs.

Mile 14.8: Three-way junction, end of pavement. To the left, the North Fork road continues upvalley. Straight ahead, road 65 crosses the North Fork on a concrete bridge, where good views can be had of mountains, river, and forest upstream, and the dark cliffs of Bear Mountain downstream. It then climbs just over 2 miles to Jack Pass on the divide between the North Fork and Beckler watersheds. From the pass, one can drive southeast on road 6550 to Evergreen Mountain (Hike 15), drive south on road 65 down the Beckler valley to meet Highway 2 in 13 miles, or go southwest up the San Juan Hill road 6570.

At 0.6 mile on road 6570, a side road goes uphill and right. There is a rough spot at the beginning, and the road can be driven or walked to a good view of the North Fork valley and the cliffs of Troublesome Mountain (see Bonus Walk 2). Road 6570 continues several more miles up San Juan Ridge before ending with no place to walk or hike to. The Skykomish district of the Forest Service in 1999 diverted watershed restoration money to do another in a series of expensive fixes to reopen this eroding road. It could have, and should have, been decommissioned. A rare chance to fix one of the major sources of sediment in the Beckler River was lost, for the sake of keeping open a little-used road to nowhere.

Mile 14.8: Turn left here to continue up the North Fork valley. The unpaved upper North Fork road cuts through a mix of second growth and old growth forest here.

Mile 16.8: Blanca Lake trailhead. See Hike 10.

Mile 17.4: Two spur roads leave the North Fork road and form a loop, a possible future campground site.

Mile 18.7: The road passes above where the North Fork plunges down to Deer Falls, a spectacular cataract far below the road, which blocks the uppermost North Fork to anadromous fish. A breezy point along the road at the top of the gorge is usually bugfree even on hot summer days. Views can be had of Troublesome Mountain and Goblin Ridge to the west.

Mile 19.3: Trailhead for West Cady Ridge and Quartz Creek (Hikes 11 and 12) and hopefully soon for the North Fork Skykomish trail. A "scenic parkway" was once proposed to go from here over Cady Pass to Lake Wenatchee. Fortunately, only 1.3 miles were built. This section has been planned for closure by the Forest Service, and this unlogged part of the valley has been proposed for inclusion in the Wild Sky Wilderness. The road will be converted to trail. For now, it may still be drivable for those with high-clearance vehicles, but it's a pleasant walk if you don't want to risk your car. Unbroken old growth forests on the slopes make for appealing vistas. Real foot trail begins at the end of the 1.3 miles, to the North Fork Sky and Pass Creek (Hikes 13 and 14).

Back on Highway 2

Mile 35–36: This section of highway has stupendous views of Mount Index, but there is no good place to pull off and enjoy them. The best looks are from westbound car windows.

Mile 37: The sometimes-unmarked Heybrook Lookout trailhead is on the north side of the road here, opposite a large entrance sign for the Mount Baker–Snoqualmie National Forest. See Hike 16.

Mile 39: Eagle Falls. Seen quickly, and hard to appreciate from a car. It is

Eagle Falls

possible, though dangerous, to park along the highway and walk down a boot-beaten path to rocks and a deep green pool below the falls.

Mile 41: Turnoff north to Barclay Lake trail, Hike 17.

Mile 45: Grotto, former site of a cement plant famous for dusting leaves in the area white.

Mile 46: Turnoff to Money Creek Campground and Old Cascade Highway.

Mile 46 Side Trip: Old Cascade Highway, Lowe Creek, Money Creek, and Miller River

The Old Cascade Highway offers a pleasant back-road approach to the town of Skykomish, and the Money Creek and Miller River roads are scenic drives to hiking possibilities in the Alpine Lakes Wilderness and environs.

Mile 0: The Old Cascade Highway crosses the South Fork Skykomish just before Highway 2 goes through a short tunnel. The road passes Money Creek Campground, located among some remnant old growth trees.

Mile 0.3: Immediately after crossing railroad tracks, a side road goes right and downstream toward Lowe Creek, a good winter walk. See Hike 18.

Mile 0.9: Miller River road 6410 turns south (right) here. Less than a tenth of a mile up it, another road turns right and west up Money Creek. Passing some cabins, this road (6420) climbs through forest for several miles before breaking out into the open. At about 5 miles are tremendous views south to Goat Basin and Lennox Mountain, one of the best car-accessible vistas in the Skykomish area. (However, it does cross an ever-changing slide area.) At about 7 miles, just before its end, the road reaches small Lake Elizabeth, encircled by a short, rather muddy trail (see Bonus Walk 3). The Money Creek road makes a good ski trip with the right snow conditions.

Miller River road 6410 heads south past the Money Creek turnoff and passes above some river channels before entering old growth forest. The Miller River Campground (a reservation-only group site) has some enormous trees. At about 3 miles, a strikingly large cedar tree can be seen off to the right. At 3.5 miles, a side road goes right to the West Fork Miller (Hike 19). The West Fork and then the East Fork Miller are crossed, and views can be had of surrounding ridges. At 9 miles, the road ends at the Lake Dorothy trailhead (Hike 20). The Miller River road is closed to snowmobiles, making it a good ski or snowshoe destination in winter.

Mile 1.3: The Old Cascade Highway crosses a fast and scenic stretch of the Miller River on an old cantilever bridge. Maloney Ridge is to the southeast.

Mile 2: "Milltown," some houses located near the site of the vanished Skykomish sawmill.

Mile 2.3: Some impressively forested slopes of Maloney Ridge can be seen ahead.

Mile 3: Town of Skykomish. Be sure to obey the 25 mph speed limit; the local sheriff lives along this stretch of road.

Mile 3.2: Maloney Creek is crossed, flowing out of a wild, trailless valley.

Mile 3.3: Junction. To the left are downtown Skykomish and Highway 2. The Old Cascade Highway continues straight ahead.

Mile 3.8: A triangular set of railroad sidings once served to turn locomotives around.

Mile 4.3: A pull-off to the right goes to a view of the Skykomish airfield.

Mile 4.7: The old highway rejoins Highway 2.

Back on Highway 2

Mile 46: The highway passes through a short tunnel. Immediately after it is a quick view south to the east summit of Lennox Mountain.

Mile 48: Town of Skykomish. Turn right (south) from the highway and cross the river on a steel bridge. Several historic structures are of interest, including the multistory hotel, which has a restaurant on the lower floor. An interesting stove restoration shop occupies the site of Maloney's store. On the railroad, in the days before diesel power, Skykomish was where electric locomotives took over from steam engines for the tunnel passage. The town is now dealing with oil wastes from the railroad works that contaminated the groundwater. Skykomish has great views northeast to Beckler Peak and northwest to Grotto Mountain. The valley of Maloney Creek to the south is almost completely wild, with no roads or trails.

Mile 49: Turnoff north to Beckler River road 65.

Mile 49 Side Trip: Beckler and Rapid River Valleys

The lower reaches of the broad Beckler River valley were railroad logged in the 1930s and are now blanketed with naturally regenerated second growth forests. The first 7 miles of road are paved and are a pleasant drive. Continuing north, a nice 30-mile loop can be driven over Jack Pass to connect with road 63 from Index.

Mile 0: The paved Beckler River road 65 heads north from Highway 2.

Mile 0.7: The Eagle Creek road climbs west about 7 miles to an unofficial trail into Eagle Lake. (See Hike 17.) This road crosses some steep failure-prone slopes and may one day cease to be maintained.

Mile 1.1: Cross Beckler River on a concrete bridge.

Mile 1.5: Beckler River Campground.

Mile 1.5–7: The Beckler River road 65 follows the river north for almost 6 pleasant miles through nice seventy-year-old forests, a rare example of a paved road that was built to sit lightly on the land.

Mile 7: End of pavement just before a four-way junction. Straight ahead, road 65 reaches Jack Pass in 6 miles, mostly through logged areas but with occasional patches of old growth. Some views can be had from the pass. The Evergreen Mountain road (Hike 15) goes southeast from Jack Pass. North of Jack Pass, road 65 descends to the North Fork Skykomish valley to meet road 63 from Index.

Another road, 6520, goes hard right from the junction at the end of pavement and starts climbing immediately; 2.7 miles up this road, reach another junction. The right fork, road 6524, descends to a crossing of Johnson Creek (the bridge may be gone), then climbs up into a moonscape of two square-mile sections that were clearcut fence to fence by Weyerhaeuser before going to the Forest Service in a land exchange. Straight ahead, road 6520 continues another 4 miles through areas logged off by the Forest Service to the trailhead for Johnson Ridge (Hike 21).

A third road, 6530, makes a less-hard right 90 degrees east of the junction at the end of pavement on the Beckler road and stays level as it starts up the little-known Rapid River valley. The road crosses the river (an important salmon stream) a number of times, traversing mostly second growth forest and some areas burned in the logging-caused Evergreen Mountain fire in 1967. At about 4.5 miles, the Meadow Creek trail is passed (Hike 22). The road then crosses the North Fork Rapid on a concrete bridge and enters old growth forest for a final mile before abruptly ending. This last mile has been proposed for inclusion in the Wild Sky Wilderness, with the road converted to trail. The Rapid River valley continues for about 6 miles beyond the road's end, wild and trailless except for the Pacific Crest Trail, which crosses its very upper end at Lake Janus (Hike 36).

Back on Highway 2

Mile 49: Just after the Beckler turnoff, the highway crosses the South Fork Skykomish. Just above the bridge is the confluence of the Beckler and Tye Rivers, which unite to form the South Fork Skykomish.

Mile 50: U.S. Forest Service Skykomish Ranger Station. Information, maps, permits. Turnoff to Foss River road.

Mile 50 Side Trip: Foss River, Tonga Ridge, Maloney Ridge

Road 68 heads south from Highway 2 into the spectacular Foss valley and the northern side of the Alpine Lakes Wilderness. Scenic, popular trails can be reached on Tonga Ridge and both forks of the Foss, and the road climbs high to broad, car-accessible views from Maloney Ridge.

Mile 0: Road 68, the Foss River road, heads south from Highway 2, passing some private cabins.

Mile 1.2: The Foss River is crossed on an old wood decked bridge. Immediately past it, keep right on road 68.

Mile 2.4: The road passes under a high railroad trestle.

Mile 3.6: Junction with Tonga Ridge road 6830, which climbs left for 7 miles to spur 310 leading to the scenic Tonga Ridge trail (Hike 23).

Mile 4.2: East Fork Foss trailhead (Hike 24). The mostly level trail traverses lovely, naturally regrown second growth forest.

Mile 4.5: Road 6835 goes left 2 miles to the West Fork Foss trailhead to numerous lakes (Hike 25).

Mile 4.5–8: The road climbs north onto Maloney Ridge with growing views.

Mile 8: Junction with road 6846 (may not be signed). Go left for about 2.5 miles to reach the trail to Evans Lake (Bonus Walk 4). It's also possible to continue on road 68 past the junction with 6846. In about a mile a spur road (210) goes right a short distance to the site of the old Maloney Lookout (3364 feet), now occupied by radio towers but still offering very good views north and west down the Skykomish valley.

Road 68 continues to near the top of Sobieski Mountain, 4400 feet, with more radio towers, but views are better from the Maloney Lookout site.

Back on Highway 2

Mile 52: Road 6066 on the left climbs to views south across the valley and to the proposed Beckler Peak trail (Hike 26).

Mile 55: The Old Cascade Highway turns off left and parallels Highway 2 for almost 5 miles on the north side of the Tye River. Some nice old growth forest can be seen about a mile and a half up it, just after crossing Martin Creek. At 2.3 miles, road 6710 goes left to the Iron Goat trail in 1.4 miles (Hike 27).

Mile 55: Alpine Falls on the Tye River is so hidden from view, few know it is there. Just before the highway crosses the Tye River there is a parking area off to the right, where a boot-beaten path can be followed to the edge of the falls.

Mile 56: Deception Falls. This is a good place to take a break from driving, with short trails and views of foaming whitewater; see Bonus Walk 5.

Mile 57: Just short of milepost 57, road 6088 goes right ¼ mile to the trailhead for Deception Creek (Hike 29).

Mile 58: The small railroad town of Scenic was once located here. A road drops right, crosses the railroad tracks, and turns right to the Surprise Creek trailhead (Hike 30). A bit farther, another segment of the Old Cascade Highway turns north. It's no longer possible to follow it all the way to Stevens Pass due to a washout.

Mile 59: As the road starts up a long grade, the west portal of the 7.9-mile Cascade Tunnel, built in 1929 and formerly the longest in North America, is passed. Electric locomotives were used to pull trains through it until 1956, when a ventilation system was installed to allow use by diesel locomotives, ending the need to switch between steam and electric locomotives. However, anyone who has staggered, gasping for

Alpine Falls, on the Tye River

air, to the door of a boxcar after riding through the tunnel behind a string of diesel engines will testify that the ventilation system leaves something to be desired.

Train whistles are a constant presence all along Highway 2, and most people find them a pleasing sound when heard from trails high above. True railroad buffs tend to scorn the Stevens Pass line, though, since almost all the traffic on it is uninteresting container trains carrying Asian cargo from the Port of Seattle to Chicago.

Mile 60: As the road passes by some impressive old growth forest, the Tunnel Creek road turns right at a horseshoe bend (accessible only from the eastbound lanes). The road accesses the Tunnel Creek trail to Hope and Mig Lakes (Hike 31).

Mile 60–62: After the horsehoe bend at Tunnel Creek, views can be had looking back down the Tye valley. The roads swings northeast, and the slopes of Windy Ridge are seen across the upper Tye valley. Much of Windy Ridge burned in railroad-caused fires a century ago and is only slowly reforesting. Extensive huckleberry and mountain ash fields turn brilliant orange and red in the fall. Views are better from the outside, westbound lanes, where from a few spots it's possible to see the snowsheds built to shelter Great Northern trains before the switch to the lower tunnel in 1929. Dark, old growth–forested slopes above Surprise Creek can also be seen when driving westbound before the road turns toward Tunnel Creek.

Mile 64: Stevens Pass. The 4061-foot high point of Highway 2 named for John F. Stevens, who engineered the first route of the Great Northern Railway over the top in 1892 and later designed the Panama Canal. Ski area and starting point for Hikes 32, 33, 34, and 35.

Mile 64–68: Highway 2 drops into the upper valley of Nason Creek. The slopes of Lichtenberg Mountain to the north were also burned in fires started by the railroad in its early years.

Mile 68: Smith Brook road 6700 turns north to Union Gap, Minotaur Lake, and Snowy Creek trailheads (Hikes 36, 37, and 39) and continues down into the Little Wenatchee valley with numerous trails and campgrounds farther north.

Mile 69: The Bygone Byways interpretive trail is just north of the road, accessible from the westbound lanes only (see Bonus Walk 6).

Mile 70: Mill Creek road 6960 goes to the Stevens Pass Nordic Center, with groomed trails. The Lanham Lake trail (Hike 38) is also found here.

East portal of the Cascade Tunnel. Quite often when driving east, blue sky will be seen ahead as one rounds a curve here looking east down the Nason Creek valley, giving promise that the clouds of the west side will be left behind.

Mile 73: Turnoff for the Rock Mountain trail, a stiff 4150-foot climb to views and meadows (Hike 39).

Mile 76: Turnoff to the trailhead for Merritt Lake and Alpine Lookout (Hikes 41 and 42).

Ray Rock Summit. The highway goes through a notch high above Nason Creek, and the westernmost ponderosa pines can be seen, the first of many to come. The northern peaks of the Chiwaukum Mountains, scarred by logging operations by the Longview Fibre Company, can be seen high across the valley to the south.

Mile 78: To the south, a road turns off and heads to the trailhead for Whitepine Creek. Not described in the trail section of this book, Whitepine Creek is a long-distance access to areas deep in the Alpine Lakes Wilderness, though it can also be day-hiked as far as time and ambition allow. About 2 miles up the trail is an unbridged crossing of Whitepine Creek, which can be problematic in early summer, but another trail branching left just before the crossing can be hiked up Wildhorse Creek through mostly open country, which burned long ago.

Mile 78–82: Lower Nason Creek valley. An eastbound driver will often break out into full sunshine here, as ponderosa pines become abundant and the land starts to have an "eastern Washington" look, smell, and feel.

Mile 79: Merritt. A road crosses Nason Creek here and goes east near and under powerlines to the trailhead for Lake Ethel. The lake itself is attractive, but the trail crosses numerous (gated) roads and extensive logged areas, making for a long (8 miles) and not very appealing walk.

Mile 82: Headed west, near a highway rest area, are views of the 7400-foot-high Chiwaukum Mountains to the left, and to the right, Rock Mountain, part of Nason Ridge.

Mile 82: A gated road across from the rest area leads to the Lake Julius trailhead. The second road (6910) on the north side of the highway to the east of the rest area leads to the eastern trailhead for Alpine Lookout (Hike 42).

Mile 85: Just short of milepost 85, state Highway 207 goes north from the Coles Corner junction to Lake Wenatchee.

MILE 85 SIDE TRIP: LAKE WENATCHEE AND BEYOND

Every guidebook has to draw a line somewhere and say "this far, and no farther." So, other than the short hike to Hidden Lake (Bonus Walk 7), no detailed information is given here about the extensive country reached by heading north on Highway 207 to Lake Wenatchee and beyond. But there are hundreds of miles of mountains and trails to be found there, and most are described in *100 Hikes in Washington's Glacier Peak Regions: The North Cascades,* by Spring and Manning, from The Mountaineers Books.

Farthest west, the Little Wenatchee trail can be followed up that valley to connect with the trail from the west to Dishpan Gap (Hike 13). Other trails there go up Lake Creek, Cady Creek, Cady Ridge, and elsewhere. The Little Wenatchee can also be reached by way of the "shortcut" route via the Smith Brook road and Rainy Pass, which leaves Highway 2 at 4 miles east of Stevens Pass (see Hikes 36 and 37).

The Smith Brook road can also be used to reach the White River trail, which traverses one of the larger, lower, forested valleys preserved in the Glacier Peak Wilderness. Other trails from the White River valley go to Mount David, to Indian Creek, and across Boulder Pass to the spectacular Napeequa Valley.

Largest, and farthest east, is the Chiwawa valley. Roads can be followed from Lake Wenatchee past Fish Lake and many miles up the Chiwawa past numerous trails and campgrounds. Trails lead to Schaefer Lake, Rock Creek, Estes Butte, Little Giant Pass, Buck Creek Pass, Chiwawa Basin, Spider Meadow, and other places as well. The Chiwawa has a drier, more open, "eastern" feel.

If all that isn't enough, even more trails can be found in the Mad River country, reached from Maverick Saddle east of Lake Wenatchee. These are almost all open to motorcycles, unfortunately, but a gate that is normally opened around August 1 keeps most of them out before then. The Mad River country has many delightful meadows and gentle summits and is well worth visiting in early summer.

Back on Highway 2

Mile 89: The Chiwaukum Creek road 7908 goes right a short ways to the Chiwaukum Creek trail (Hike 43).

Mile 90: Tumwater Campground is on the left, and to the right a road climbs the Hatchery Creek valley to the Lake Augusta trail into the Alpine Lakes Wilderness.

Highway 2 crosses the Wenatchee River and enters the scenic Tumwater Canyon.

Mile 92: Swift Water Picnic Area. Views of the Wenatchee River, picnic sites, and a short trail leading to an interesting natural rock shelter believed to have once been used by Native Americans when they fished the formerly abundant salmon runs of the Wenatchee.

Mile 92.5: Tumwater Botanic Area. A gated road provides chances to see springtime flowers and hike to the top of Tumwater Ridge; see Bonus Walk 8.

Mile 93–99: The Tumwater Canyon was the scene of extensive fires in 1994, the evidence of which can be seen all along here. Highway 2 follows closely above the Wenatchee River, where numerous stretches of white water put on quite a show during peak run-off in June.

Mile 95: Wenatchee River dam. A viewpoint provides historical details of the dam built in 1909 to supply power to electric locomotives of the Great Northern, until diesels brought the era of electric and steam engines to a close in 1956.

Mile 97: Castle Rock. A popular rock climbing spot. A trail has been constructed up the north side of the rock, which reaches a viewpoint about 200 feet up before climbing farther to the top of the rock. Views can be had down to the river and across to the forest blackened by fire in 1994.

Mile 98: A steel bridge, which once carried a pipeline supplying a generating station for electric locomotives, now serves as a footbridge and access to a good short walk (Hike 44).

Mile 99: Highway 2 leaves the Tumwater canyon and enters Leavenworth. Icicle Creek road turns south.

Mile 99 Side Trip: Icicle Valley

Until the 1960s, the Icicle valley had only a narrow dirt road winding through miles of big "yellowbelly" ponderosa pines. But the road was widened and paved, most of the big trees were hauled away, and a century of fire suppression set the stage for fires in 1994, which burned much of the lower and middle valley. Despite all this, it's still a beautiful place, with mountains rising high above the low valley floor. A number of popular trails reach scenic destinations.

Mile 0: The Icicle Creek road turns south from Highway 2 and heads up the once-rural lower Icicle valley, now a land of ranchettes.

Mile 1–9: Fires in 1994 burned much of the Icicle valley. Subsequent salvage logging by the Forest Service removed many of the best green trees, including many big, healthy ponderosa pines—trees that survived the fires, are adapted to fire, and need fire to suppress competing trees. This kind of salvage logging has been likened to "mugging a burn victim."

Mile 1.4: A bit of old road jogs to the right to the east Icicle Ridge trailhead (Hike 45).

Mile 4: Snow Lakes and Enchantment Lakes trailhead, to one of the more beautiful and most crowded places in the Cascades (Hike 47).

Mile 5–6: The road cuts across the hillside not far above Icicle Creek. To the south, Edward Peak rises to over 7000 feet, while Icicle Creek is only 1600 feet, a rise of 5400 feet in less than 2 miles, a relief matched by few other mountain ranges in the world.

Mile 7.5: Eightmile Campground.

Mile 8.5: Eightmile Creek road, access to trails to Lakes Eightmile, Caroline, Stuart, and Colchuck. See Hikes 47, 48, 49, and 50.

Mile 9.4: Fourth of July Creek trail (Hike 51), a steep climb to Icicle Ridge.

Mile 10–14: Most of the forests on both sides of the valley have been logged, but it's still nice. Pass Johnny Creek and Ida Creek Campgrounds.

Mile 15.3: Chatter Creek Campground.

Mile 15.6: Turnoff right to Chatter Creek trail (Hike 53).

Mile 15.8: Parking for Icicle Gorge trail (Hike 52).

Mile 17.5: Rock Island Campground. Roads continue up both sides of the creek; cross the bridge to the south side road. A tenth of a mile past the bridge, a road goes left 0.2 mile to the Jack Creek trail, a long-distance access up a forested valley into the Alpine Lakes Wilderness, not described in the hikes section of this volume. A mile up the Jack Creek trail, another trail branches right to Trout Creek and Trout Lake.

Mile 18: Black Pine Campground and horse loading area, trailhead for Blackjack Ridge (Hike 54).

Mile 19: Road's end and the Icicle Creek trailhead (Hike 55).

BACK ON HIGHWAY 2

Mile 99–100: Leavenworth. Many motels, shops, and restaurants. The entire town has been done up in an ersatz Bavarian village style, taken to a degree that one would be hard pressed to find anywhere in Germany. The town center is quite pleasant, with shade trees and a green park adding nice touches, making it a good place to stop and wander around, at least when there's no oompah music booming from the loudspeakers. Some of the restaurants are good (fortunately, they know better than to offer much German food). The gingerbread trim does little to disguise the ugliness of the big box motels on the west side of the town.

Although there are high, rocky mountains visible to the south, most of the dryish surrounding landscape is distinctly un-Bavarian. One wonders what the real Germans think—though apparently there are a few tourist traps in Germany that have adopted a Wild West motif. Whether it has been because of or in spite of the gingerbread, once-dying Leavenworth has put itself on the map as a major tourist destination. Interesting country beckons in all directions. A city park along the Wenatchee River has trails, shady trees to relax under, and launching facilities for early summer river rafting.

The junction of Icicle Creek and the Wenatchee River was once the site of the Wenatchepam fishery, where Native Americans caught thousands of salmon in the days before dams diminished the Columbia River runs to a trickle. The U.S. government promised the Wenatchi tribe a reservation here, but they were instead exiled to the faraway Colville reservation once whites started coveting their land. The Wenatchis are still together as a tribe and continue the quest for their promised reservation to this day.

Mile 100: Leavenworth Ranger Station, north of the highway. Maps, information, and permits.

Mile 101–117: The Wenatchee valley. Fruit orchards occupy many of the lower areas here, with pine-dotted hillsides above. Low, gentle slopes are the best locations for fruit trees, since they tend to be a few degrees warmer than valley bottoms, where freezing air gathers. Those few degrees can mean the difference between profit and disaster for growers. Where there are no orchards, one can see an abundance of "sagebrush." Three different species grow here: bitterbrush, rabbitbrush, and "true" sagebrush. Rabbitbrush and sagebrush both have yellow flowers in late summer, usually September.

Mile 105: Just before milepost 105 is the junction with U.S. Highway 97. To the south is the turnoff for the Ingalls Creek trail in about 8 miles, then Swauk Pass, Cle Elum, and Interstate 90. Heading east, Highway 2 grows to four lanes. Watch the speed limit carefully; this is a training area for State Patrol cadets, and they don't teach them to be sympathetic to fast drivers.

Mile 109: The Peshastin Pinnacles (also called the Cashmere Crags) are visible north of the highway (see Bonus Walk 10).

SIDE TRIPS: BACK ROADS OF THE WENATCHEE VALLEY

From much of the Wenatchee valley, gently sloping hills with open groves of pine trees and grassy areas stretch north and south, an appealing savannahlike landscape inviting exploration, especially in spring when clouds blanket the west side of the Cascades and snow covers the mountains. There are almost no formal trails, but much of the country is so open that there is no real need for them. Land ownership is a mix of national forest, state land, and a few private holdings. In places away from houses and other areas that might be posted against trespassing, there's nothing to prevent one from parking the car and wandering off in search of pleasantness—but watch for ticks in springtime.

The way to reach this country is on the extensive network of back roads, most of which are open and some of which can be driven by a careful driver in a regular (as opposed to a four-wheel-drive) car. The indispensable tool is a good map. The Forest Service recreation map of the Wenatchee National Forest shows just about all of the roads, and the district maps that can be purchased at ranger stations offer even more detail. No detailed directions are given here since this country could easily fill a guidebook just on its own, but a few of the places worth visiting are Chumstick and Sugarloaf Lookouts north of Highway 2; Horselake Mountain and the dramatic Liberty–Beehive road on Mission Ridge south of the highway; and the vast Colockum country along and above the Columbia River south of Wenatchee. The authors recommend a full tank of gas, a good map, and a willingness to take a few wrong turns, most of which will soon become apparent by paying attention to the map. There are hundreds of square miles of little-known terrain to explore. Park the car and get out and walk wherever it looks good.

Back on Highway 2

Mile 112: Cashmere. The historic downtown is worth a visit. A road leads south about 10 miles up Mission Creek to the Devils Gulch trail.

Mile 115.5: Wenatchee Valley County Park. Noisy camping along the highway.

Mile 118: Exit right to continue on Highway 2, which makes a three-quarter circle turn under itself to reach the bridge across the Columbia. Route 285 continues straight ahead into Wenatchee.

Mile 119: Turn right and follow signs for Wenatchee Confluence State Park, where trails offer access to wetlands and forest where the Wenatchee joins the reservoired Columbia.

Mile 120: Highway 2 crosses the Columbia, held back in a reservoir behind Rock Island dam.

Mile 128: A left turn at a traffic light leads one north on Highway 2. Good views west to the Stuart Range, Mount Cashmere, and Icicle Ridge. The highway mileage suddenly jumps by 8 miles, harkening back to the days before the Columbia was bridged here and Highway 2 ran 8 long miles south into Wenatchee and back north through East Wenatchee to reach this point. The highway follows the Columbia reservoirs north 12 miles to Orondo, passing Rocky Reach dam along the way.

Mile 140: Orondo. Highway 2 splits right from Highway 97 and climbs 6 miles up the scenic Corbaley Canyon, where pine and fir woodland covers the north-facing slopes to the right. These trees are an especially pleasing sight for westbound travelers, the first taste of the great forests of the Cascades, coming as they do after many treeless miles to the east.

Mile 146: Highway 2 tops out at 2812 feet on the western edge of the airy Waterville Plateau, once a grassland where herds of antelope ranged, now a checkerboard of wheat fields.

Mile 148: Views ahead of the city of Waterville.

Mile 150: Waterville. This is the kind of unpretentious town that is all too rare these days. The historic Waterville Hotel has been restored and is open for business, and makes a great base for a bike trip. The nearly empty county roads, many of them paved and following square-mile section lines across the wheat fields, are ideal for biking. A Metsker map of Douglas County is useful. From the breezy high points on the plateau one can see a lot of sky, with the Cascades to the west stretching from the Stuart Range in the south to Sugarloaf Mountain straight west, and north to the low defile of Maverick Saddle. Farther right and north are Tyee Ridge, then Stormy Mountain above Lake Chelan. An open and spacious country, where "the air nimbly recommends itself, and pleases the senses."

Mile 150+: Highway 2 continues east across plains and mountains to the infinite, mysterious East.

Opposite: *Mount Baring from Mount Persis* Photo by John Roper

THE WILD SKY MOUNTAINS

Sky Peaks and Ragged Ridge

Highway 2 cuts across the Central Cascades, topping out at Stevens Pass, elevation 4056 feet. The areas west of the pass, in the Skykomish River watershed, have become known as the Wild Sky country; areas east of the pass are generally known as Wenatchee country. The fifty-five hikes and ten shorter walks described in this book, all of them close to Highway 2, offer trails for every taste, from short forest nature walks to strenuous all-day climbs to high viewpoints, from lush green forests in the west to the dry sagebrush-and-pine, blue-sky country in the east. Few other places so close to major population centers offer so much wild country, and with such a variety of trails and landscapes, this book offers nearly endless opportunities for hiking exploration. The following pages highlight some of the more interesting aspects of the lands, forests, wildlife, and history of the areas described in this book.

Mountains and Valleys

The Central Cascades are a fascinating place. The dramatic physical relief, combined with extensive stretches of wild, biologically productive forests, is matched few places on Earth. This is where the Canadian-sized mountains meet the rich Oregon type of forests. North of the Cascades, the British Columbia Coast Range is a land of large icecaps and glaciers where the climate is colder, species fewer, and trees generally smaller. The South Cascades, which really extend from Interstate 90 south, are a floristically rich land of warm summers, big trees, and mostly gentle mountains.

But this friendlier southern terrain doesn't have the kind of natural obstacles to roadbuilding and logging that have helped protect areas to the north, and very little of the southern region has survived intact. Thus the North and Central Cascades have been described as the perfect mix: far enough north to have enough snow and ice to make things interesting, but not smothered by icecaps. Mountainous enough to be impressively scenic and to have kept roads from being built everywhere, but not so steep as to make foot travel and trailbuilding very difficult. And far enough south to encompass the reliably warm summers and botanic richness not found to the north. Combined with the natural diversity arising from having both a wet (west) and a dry (east) side, it all adds up to a pleasing marriage of north and south, east and west, a place where these different influences meet and blend attractively.

The Cascades are not particularly old, as mountains go. The mountains we see were formed mostly within the last six million years or so. The volcanoes are quite young compared to the rest of the range and are still works in progress, as Mount St. Helens reminded everyone in 1980. Many volumes have been written about how the various plates, faults, plutons, intrusions, batholiths, et cetera, have come together to form the rocky bones of the Cascades. Suffice it to say here that the Cascades have been called one of the most geologically diverse mountain ranges in the world, where

Eagle Lake (Hike 17) from Mount Townsend; Merchant Peak to the right, Mount Index behind left Photo by Mark Lawler

just about every kind of rock can be found. Surprisingly, there is an almost total lack of minerals here that can be profitably mined. Legend has it that of all the mines operated in this area, only the Sunset Mine (Hike 7) ever turned a profit. Although the acid drainage from some of these old mines is still a problem, the Cascades have been mostly spared the kind of river-poisoning, toxic-mining legacy that blights parts of the Rockies. A great place for rock hounds; not so good for prospectors.

Though not high compared to other mountains, the Cascades look and feel very high because they rise from very low valleys. It's this immense local relief that makes them so dramatically "mountainous." A couple of examples in the area covered by this guidebook: From the South Fork Skykomish River, elevation 500 feet, Mount Index rises to just under 6000 feet in the space of 2 miles, about 2750 feet per mile. Near Leavenworth, Edward Peak rises to over 7000 feet less than 2 miles from Icicle Creek, at an elevation of 1600 feet—about 3000 feet per mile. Many other much higher mountain ranges have nowhere near this kind of relief.

Climate

The abrupt mountain wall of the Cascades greatly affects local climates. Moist air masses moving off the Pacific Ocean rise and cool as they encounter the Cascades, wringing water out of the clouds. On many a sunny afternoon along Puget Sound, the view east is of a wall of gray. From 35 inches per year at Seattle, rainfall levels rise rapidly heading toward the mountains to 80 inches at the town of Index and as much as 190 inches on some of the higher west-side mountains. Farther east, levels drop to around 80 inches at Stevens Pass, 25 inches at Leavenworth, and 10 inches at Wenatchee. From the lush west to the arid east, the look and character of the landscapes are determined largely by rainfall amounts.

The pattern of Cascades rainfall is seasonal, falling mostly from late October to May. Snowline varies with temperature, with areas above 2000 feet experiencing considerable snowfall most winters. The snow levels reported in weather forecasts tend to be accurate for the western mountain front only. Farther into the mountains the snowline generally will be lower, and valleys that penetrate the mountains deeply will receive much heavier snowfalls than their low elevations might suggest. Quite often a big dump of snow will come early, even in October, only to be followed by warmer weather and heavy rain. These "rain on snow" events can release huge volumes of water, causing serious flooding. Maintaining the forest cover is critical to controlling this run-off.

The seasons themselves tend to occur later in the marine-influenced Cascades than in other climates, since it takes a long time for ocean waters to heat and cool. This means that real summer often doesn't start until sometime in July but can extend into October. Winter is similarly delayed, with the heaviest snow accumulations not seen until March or even April.

Snowshoer on Mineral Butte (Hike 8) Photo by Rick McGuire

Springtime is the longest season in the Cascades, with showery weather punctuated by sun breaks in low wetlands and deep snows in the higher mountains. Skiing and snowshoeing are at their best at this time of year, and snow covers brush, making for easy travel.

Another weather phenomenon of interest to hikers is the "marine layer," clouds that can occur during periods of high-pressure weather. Forming when warm air rises, drawing in moist air from the ocean, these "good-weather" clouds seldom produce much rain but do bring significant moisture to the forests through fog drip. They have been cursed by many a west-sider for cheating the area out of some of its best summer weather. Sometimes they extend east only as far as the western front of the range, and a driver heading east from Gold Bar will suddenly burst into sunshine. At other times they will extend all the way to the crest or even 5 to 10 miles beyond. Usually these clouds burn off by midday or soon after, but they can last all day. Weather reports are seldom of much use in gauging how high up and how far east these clouds will reach; "morning clouds, lower west slopes" is about as specific as they get. When marine clouds roll in, hikers in search of sun have two options: They can drive east, confident that at some point the clouds will be left behind. Or they can keep the faith and head up the trail into the gray. Often the cloud tops will be found between 2000 and 4000 feet. There are few experiences to match the joy of climbing out of the gloom into the sunshine, looking down to a sea of clouds below.

Weather forecasting in the Cascades, though greatly improved in recent years, is still a difficult art. Fronts can arrive daily during winter. Although every year sees stretches of clear winter skies, there are inevitably long periods of dark, gray, rainy weather. Combined with the short winter days, this can make the wintertime Cascades a poor place for those who crave light and sun, especially during December and January. But by the first of February, the days are growing noticeably longer and the "Big Dark" is losing its grip. Although winter weather patterns commonly persist into April, rapidly lengthening days soon make the gloom of winter a distant memory, more than compensated for by the long days of spring and summer. The sun is up sixteen hours a day in June and July, sunlight bathes even the north-facing slopes, and the endless evening twilights linger until after 10:00 P.M.

Forests

"Ours was once a forested planet"—particularly this part of it, which still is. The scale and richness of the forests are what set the Cascades apart from other mountains. Many ranges have higher or more spectacular peaks; none, excepting perhaps the Olympics, have more spectacular forests. The west-side Cascade forests are part of the great arc of temperate rain forest that until recently stretched from the California redwoods north to Prince William Sound in southern Alaska.

Old growth forest, Howard Creek Photo by Mark Lawler

Logging has consumed most of the lower-elevation old growth, or "ancient" forest, that blanketed the Skykomish valleys and parts of the east side of the Cascades, but significant areas remain. In places such as Troublesome Creek, along the Blanca Lake trail, and the lower West Cady Ridge trail (Bonus Walk 1 and Hikes 10 and 11), one can see fine examples of the original Cascade forests. The size and character of the trees, and the richness of moss and lichens and understory, never fail to impress. Although there is no single, agreed-upon scientific definition of "old growth," it is generally taken to mean a forest that has never been logged. Ancient forests have a certain something about them—more than just the large trees, or the profusion of mosses—that strikes a chord somewhere deep inside. Perhaps it has something to do with the fact that humans have lived near and among such settings for 99 percent of the time we've been on this planet. Whatever it is, you know it when you see it, and old growth forests look like forests *should* look.

In the Skykomish region, Douglas fir is the most impressive tree. Prevalent at elevations below 3000 feet and favoring south and west exposures and well-drained soils, some trees reach over 250 feet in height and 8 or more feet in diameter. One especially large individual, nearly 11 feet thick, can be seen along the West Fork Foss trail below Trout Lake (Hike 25). Old growth Douglas fir has been called the finest lumber tree in the world, and was almost the only species sought after in the early days of logging here. The strong, easily worked wood is also very decay resistant. Consequently, old growth Douglas fir forests are scarce these days, but they do survive in a number of areas in the Skykomish. These forests tend to be comparatively brushfree and are the ones that most often have the classic "cathedral" look enjoyed by forest admirers.

If Douglas fir is the king of the forests, then the queen is western red cedar, with its graceful, feminine beauty a nice counterpoint to Douglas fir. The biggest known cedars in the Skykomish approach 14 feet in diameter, usually with multiple "picklefork" tops. Some excellent specimens can be seen along the Miller River road and the West Fork Miller trail (Hike 19). Completing the big three is western hemlock. Though seldom attaining the individual stature of Douglas fir or cedar, it makes up for it with ubiquity and is found throughout every forest except those near timberline. At middle and higher elevations, shade-tolerant Pacific silver fir is abundant. Forests of silver fir and hemlock comprise most of the old growth acreage found in the Skykomish. These forests often have a dark, mysterious air, especially on cloudy spring days when varied thrushes sound their melancholy note.

Mountain hemlock is the signature tree of the snowy, upper forests, sometimes attaining surprisingly large size. It often forms "islands" among heather and flower meadows, accompanied by subalpine fir. Alaska, or yellow cedar, is another stately tree of the upper forests. It is perhaps the longest lived of any tree in the Skykomish forests, and can survive 1500 years or more. Many Alaska cedars can be found near and below Eagle Lake (Hike 17). Noble fir is recognizable by the bluish cast of its foliage and its very regular, geometric branching pattern. It reaches the northern limit of its range here, with some trees found along Johnson Ridge (Hike 21) and a few other spots, including along Highway 2 near and above Tunnel Creek. It's been speculated that this species is still in the process of moving north after the most recent Ice Age. Lodgepole pine is often seen on dry rocky sites, and western white pine is widespread throughout all areas, though never abundant. A few Sitka spruces grow in moist lower areas, such as along the lower Lake Serene trail (Hike 6).

Deciduous trees comprise a significant part of the Skykomish forests. Red alder is well known as a pioneer tree able to colonize tough sites and, thanks to fungi that live in its roots, fix nitrogen from the air and restore the most degraded places. Any road not driven on regularly is usually taken over by alders in the space of a year or two. Black cottonwood grows profusely on lower slopes and along river bottoms, sometimes reaching 175 feet in height. Big-leaf maple is perhaps the most impressive of all the deciduous trees, with large, spreading, moss-draped specimens found in many of the lower old growth and second growth forests. Its large limbs can support veritable gardens of mosses, ferns, and flowering plants, and

Second growth forest, North Fork Skykomish valley Photo by Kevin Geraghty

maples will grow rootlets off their limbs to absorb nutrients from the aerial soils thus formed.

Although ancient forests project a sense of timelessness and permanence, these forests are in fact constantly changing and evolving. Individual species of trees migrate, not communities, and the forests we see today are only the latest mix in an ongoing process. Just in the 10,000 or so years since the continental ice sheets left the Central Cascades and nearby lowlands, there have been many changes. Lodgepole pine is believed to have formed the first forests that followed the ice sheets. During a period called the "hypsithermal" about 6000 years ago, the climate was much warmer and drier than today and there were few or no glaciers in the Cascades. The Puget Sound lowlands are believed to have been a savannah-like mix of grassland with islands of Douglas fir, perhaps like that seen in the drier parts of the San Juan Islands today. There is no such thing as a "normal" climate—it's always changing. Most old growth forests we see today began growing during the "little ice age" of A.D. 1400–1750, when the Cascades climate was considerably colder and drier than now. Most observers believe the past century has been comparatively warm and wet, with much faster tree growth than preceding centuries.

In addition to old growth forests, the lower valleys of the Skykomish hold extensive areas of maturing, naturally regenerated second growth forests that grew back spontaneously following early day railroad logging. This early logging was far different than the modern industrial logging of today. Only the best trees were transported out, and much biological legacy remained. No effort was made to artificially replant nursery-grown trees, and a diverse forest of Douglas fir, cedar, hemlock, alder, maple, and cottonwood has come back on its own. The low valleys where these forests have regrown are some of the most productive sites in the entire national forest system. These seventy- to eighty-five-year-old forests have many trees 2 to 3 feet in diameter and approaching 150 feet in height. Appearing quite natural, if left alone they will grow into old growth in little more than the span of a human lifetime from now.

Almost all of the salmon-spawning areas are surrounded by these maturing forests, and they are critical for watershed protection. The lower North Fork Skykomish and Beckler valleys, in particular, are covered by these forests, and from high vantage points they can be seen forming a continuous, unbroken blanket. The value of these lowland forests has been recognized by the authors of the Wild Sky Wilderness bill, which proposes to protect many of these areas, a major change from previous wilderness bills, which have protected mostly higher-elevation lands.

As one moves east over Stevens Pass, the forests change little at first, since the marine influence can extend for some miles east of the crest. But soon there are fewer hemlock and silver fir trees, with grand fir taking their place. Descending into the valley of Nason Creek, one notices the first ponderosa pines; these trees become more dominant the farther east one goes. Stately ponderosa pines give the areas around Leavenworth a classic "western" feel.

A century ago, open grassy forests of tall ponderosa pines covered much of the lower Wenatchee River valley, and it is said that a wagon or a Model T easily could be driven for miles through these parklike woodlands. Frequent light ground fires, often set by Native Americans, kept these forests free of underbrush, seldom damaging the large, thick-barked, fire-resistant pines. The low density of the forests, with relatively few trees per acre competing with each other, ensured that there was plenty of water and nutrients to go around and kept the forest healthy. With the arrival of Europeans, the burning practices of the Indians were halted, and fire was viewed as the enemy. In what is now seen as a mistake of monumental proportions, a fire suppression system stopped the natural burning cycle and allowed an unnatural buildup of downed wood, flammable underbrush, and small trees—a dangerous fuel load that now gravely threatens these forests, since any fires that start now can quickly flare up to catastrophic dimensions. The evidence of this can be seen from Highway 2 in

Tumwater Canyon and in the Icicle Creek valley near Leavenworth, where serious fires in 1994 closed the highway, threatened the town, and caused damage far beyond what was considered normal before the fuel buildup.

Unlike west-side forests, where fires are rare, the flammability of east-side forests is a big problem with no easy solution. The Forest Service and state authorities recognize the problem, and some fuel reduction projects have begun. An inherent problem is that there are no markets for, and no good way to dispose of, the small-diameter materials that need to be removed. Taking out the larger, fire-resistant trees is what pays, but this only worsens the problem. The timber industry and its allies have attempted to use fire danger as a smokescreen to log the bigger trees. If they succeed, it will only make a bad situation much worse. What's needed is a comprehensive program to reduce fuels in the areas near houses and towns through cleaning up downed wood, thinning out small trees and brush, and pruning off lower limbs of trees that stay, possibly with careful use of controlled burning afterward and an acceptance that many backcountry fires will be uncontrollable and will have to run their course.

Meadows

Meadowlands crown many of the higher mountains. Where the high western front of the range catches every cloud, heather meadows predominate. Low-growing heathers and dwarf berry bushes blend with islands of mountain hemlock trees to form scenic alpine parklands, often interspersed with small grassy areas and tarns. A good place to see this kind of country is on Mineral Butte (Hike 8).

A little farther inland where it's a bit sunnier are what botanists call "grass/forb" meadows. These are the delightful, classic, emerald-green "flower" meadows so attractive to hikers. They can be seen in places such as West Cady Ridge (Hike 11) and Dishpan Gap (Hike 13). A profusion of herbaceous plants grows in these meadows, with anemones, lupines, mountain bistort, Indian paintbrush, and the magnificent tiger lily competing for space. One of the most common plants is Sitka valerian, the wonderful pungent odor of which fills the air on warm days. These meadows are the scene of intense activity by pollinating insects such as bumblebees and an abundance of syrphid, or "hover" flies. These small yellow-and-black flies are often mistaken for bees or wasps, but they neither bite nor sting. Their name comes from their tendency to hover perfectly still, their wings producing a high-pitched whine. They will often land harmlessly on an arm or leg (don't swat them!) and are the most important pollinators in the Cascades.

A third type of meadows are the moist, sometimes boggy "low" meadows that can be found in places such as Paradise Meadow near Eagle Lake (Hike 17) and near the confluence of Pass Creek and the North Fork Skykomish (Hike 13). Here, plants such as coltsfoot, skunk cabbage, and cow parsnip provide food in early spring for wildlife at a critical time when higher elevations are still snow covered. Some of these meadows are home to the carnivorous sundew plant, which traps insects in its sticky jaws, and up to five species of rare orchids.

Fish and Wildlife

Seekers of charismatic megafauna will do better in Yellowstone Park than the Cascades. The west-side forests have always been noted more for silence than for an abundance of wildlife, and the dense vegetation can make it difficult to see what wildlife there is. The more open east-side forests generally offer better wildlife viewing, as do the alpine meadows in summer. Deer are numerous on the east side, less so on the west side, and can be a very unwelcome sight in one's headlights around dusk. A few elk inhabit the area. Probably the most commonly seen animal is the Douglas squirrel, much given to loudly scolding uninvited human guests. A lucky hiker might occasionally catch a glimpse of a flying squirrel, a preferred food of the endangered spotted owl, gliding silently from tree to tree. Open rocky areas are frequented by pikas, or "coneys" (see Coney Basin, Hike 19). Marmots are plentiful in high alpine basins, where their shrill alarm whistle can often be heard.

If one animal could be said to symbolize the Skykomish area, it would be the mountain goat, the emblem of the Great Northern Railway that first crossed Stevens Pass in 1893. Most high ridges and passes have goat trails along or through them, and many a climber has solved a routefinding problem by following their paths. Mountain goats really live up to their name and feel safest on the kind of vertical terrain where people feel most unsafe. Their alacrity and surefootedness are amazing. In summer they disperse across the range, but in winter they tend to congregate on steep south-facing slopes that shed snow, exposing food plants. One good place to look for them is from the Bear Mountain viewpoint above Jack Pass (Bonus Walk 2). With binoculars or a spotting scope one can sometimes see goats across the valley on the slopes of Troublesome Mountain, where they gather in snowy winters. The mountain goat population in the Skykomish–Darrington area has fallen in recent years. No one knows quite why, though disease is suspected. They remain abundant in areas farther north, and it's hoped that the Skykomish population will recover.

Marmot sunbathing on a rock

Wolverines still inhabit the Cascades, in very small numbers. In 2002 one was confirmed with an

Mountain goats are common near Alpine Baldy Lookout, on Nason Ridge.

automatic camera south of Highway 2. Cougars are on the comeback, with more sightings in the past decade than in most of the preceding century. The easing of hunting pressure has allowed their numbers to rebound, and no one fortunate enough to see their fluid movements will ever forget it. The Sultan Basin and western foothill areas seem to hold the most cougars. Their smaller cousin, the bobcat, is also around in fair numbers, and has no qualms about indulging in a semicannibalistic lunch of domestic house cat.

Coyotes eat anything and range all through western Washington, from Seattle to the Cascade crest. Their big brother, the timber wolf, was trapped and hunted relentlessly early in the past century, and was extirpated from the Cascades. Wolves have moved back into Washington from British Columbia in recent years, and though their numbers are still quite small, they really are here. As their numbers increase, so do the chances for a camper in the Cascades to thrill to the sound of their howls on a moonlit night.

Black bears are abundant in the Cascades, and anyone who hikes high meadows in summer and fall will see one sooner or later. They depend on berries to fatten up for winter. Unless challenged by a dog they want nothing to do with people and will do their best to avoid contact. Their larger relative, the grizzly, is another returnee coming home from Canada. Grizzlies lived in the Cascades and eastern Washington but for unknown reasons were rare in the Puget Sound lowlands before European settlement. Persecuted relentlessly, one of the last was killed in 1965 in what is now North Cascades National Park. But, along with wolves, they survived in British Columbia, and in recent years have begun to filter back south and reoccupy their home range in the Cascades.

There have been a number of grizzly sightings in recent years and confirmed evidence as far south as Mount Rainier. Grizzlies have large home ranges, covering hundreds of miles. They are "human intolerant," and will go to extreme lengths to avoid people. Their primary need is for undisturbed habitat. Fortunately, the Skykomish and other parts of the Cascades north of I-90 do have such places. The Forest Service, Park Service, and U.S. Fish and Wildlife Service have designated the Cascades north of I-90 as a grizzly bear recovery area and have taken steps to protect "core security habitat," the interiors of the roadless and trailless areas, both inside and outside designated wilderness This will help keep the Cascades the kind of place grizzlies can come back home to.

The Skykomish river system is one of the best remaining strongholds of anadromous fish—those species that spawn in freshwater but spend most of their lives in saltwater—in the Puget Sound Basin. Many miles of spawning and rearing habitat are present, and it is a source of clear, cold water for downstream spawning areas. The greatest extent of spawning grounds is below the mountains, especially in the "braided channel" reach between Sultan and Gold Bar. There are also important areas upstream. The North Fork Skykomish is unique among Cascade rivers in that anadromous fish can ascend it to within 5 miles of the crest, where Deer Falls, elevation 2100 feet, blocks passage.

These high mountain spawning areas are perfect for bull trout, or Dolly Varden, a threatened species that is losing ground in many places but doing well on the North Fork. Bull trout need clear, cold water to spawn, no warmer than 2 degrees centigrade. The upper North Fork is also home to the best-known anadromous fish in the Skykomish country, the steelhead. Steelhead are strong swimmers and often go far up streams and falls that can stop salmon. They do not necessarily die after spawning. One place to view them is the rocky gorge of Troublesome Creek (Bonus Walk 1), where a lucky visitor might catch a glimpse of one making the impossible-looking ascent of the falls against a mountain of water.

Three species of salmon are commonly found in the North Fork. Chinook, another threatened species, spawn in the lower North Fork near Index. Coho, or silver salmon, which are not threatened, are also present. These are considered by many to be the most flavorful salmon, though they are best when caught in saltwater rather than fresh, where they burn up all their fat stores reaching spawning grounds. Pink salmon can be especially abundant and run in odd-numbered years. They can often be seen in October in the lower Sultan River, or in the North Fork Sky at Index. Spawned-out salmon are an important source of nutrients for wildlife and benefit the whole ecosystem.

Salmon and steelhead are naturally blocked from reaching the South Fork Skykomish Basin by Sunset, Canyon, and Eagle Falls. Since the late 1950s, the Washington Department of Fish and Wildlife has operated a trap and haul facility to transport fish around the falls, opening up more than 120 miles of spawning grounds that anadromous fish never naturally reached. Bull trout, steelhead, and salmon now spawn in these waters, reproducing naturally apart from the "fish taxi." Although this has increased angling opportunities, it did have some negative effects on the resident, non-anadromous fish. Eagles once nested on the South Fork and fed on

Summer steelheading, North Fork Skykomish River Photo by Bob Heirman

resident fish. They no longer do so, but instead now scavenge salmon carcasses in fall and winter. This contributed to a change in thinking among fisheries managers, which has so far kept similar facilities from being built on rivers such as the Snoqualmie, above Snoqualmie Falls. Lowe Creek (Hike 18) is a good place to view South Fork chum and coho in late fall and early winter.

The Central Cascades are justly famous for the alpine lakes for which the wilderness area is named. Most of these lakes are above migration barriers and were thus naturally barren of fish. For the past century they have been stocked with fish by the state and by private groups and individuals. Fish reproduce naturally in some of the larger lakes, but most populations remain dependent on continued restocking. Some lakes, especially more remote ones far from trails, offer excellent fishing. Native amphibians, including frogs and salamanders, have declined due to competition and predation from these non-native fish.

People and Politics

Native Americans lived in the Skykomish area for many thousands of years before the arrival of Europeans, and it's thought that they occupied the area not long after the retreat of the Ice Age glaciers. Not many details are known about their use of the Skykomish–Stevens Pass area and the lands to the east. It was once a widely held myth that the Indians shunned the mountains and lived almost exclusively in the lowlands. This was not the case. They gathered berries in late summer, sought out the best rocks for fashioning into arrow points, and hunted and even trapped mountain goats, the hides of which were prized for their warmth. Native Americans ranged over the length and breadth of the Cascades. Though they may not have been peak-baggers in the modern sense of the term, it's clear that they were intimately familiar with the land that supported them, and in ways that we can scarcely imagine today. Their world and every part of it was a living place for them. They lived sustainably and successfully for millennia without damaging their home. Every major mountain and creek had an Indian name. This was not an empty country when the first Europeans arrived.

Although the Indians used the entire area, their major, semipermanent dwellings were in the lowlands, mostly along rivers and near good fishing spots. A major habitation was at the confluence of the Sultan and Skykomish Rivers, where Indians lived within the memory of people alive today. They traveled by canoe as far up the rivers as possible and used trails in the upper valleys where canoe travel was impracticable. Trade and family ties connected coastal and interior peoples. Their main route across the Cascades was south of the Skykomish valley, from the upper Snoqualmie at North Bend through the Cedar River valley and across the crest into the upper Yakima drainage. Another route ascended the North Fork Skykomish to Cady Pass (Hike 14) and down to Lake Wenatchee.

The early history of contact between the natives and Europeans was not a happy one. The Europeans arrived with modern weapons and an army of infectious microbes. A smallpox epidemic in 1838 killed a large percentage of the Skykomish people. The natives were given little choice about signing very unfavorable treaties, and most of the surviving Skykomish bands were relocated downstream to the Tulalip Indian Reservation, at the mouth of the Snohomish River. Some refused to go and continued to live in their home places. They had a difficult time sustaining themselves without land titles in the face of overwhelming numbers of whites, since they were unable to "own" land in the same way that whites could. Some individuals and groups were tolerated for a while, but whenever the new "owners" found their presence inconvenient, they called in the federal Indian agents, who gave the natives the choice of the reservation or prison. By 1930 the last few holdouts were gone. Thus ended the many thousands of years of Skykomish people living in the Cascades.

The removal of the natives was morally indefensible and is increasingly seen as legally indefensible as well. Native culture survived, though, and native people have mounted a legal counterattack. The Boldt decision in 1974 and subsequent rulings have reaffirmed not only native rights to half of fish and shellfish harvests, but also rights to protection of the environment that supports the fisheries. These cases are likely only the first rounds in what may ultimately grow into a much broader redress of old wrongs. The Tulalip tribes have played an important part in protecting the lands and waters of the Skykomish Basin and will continue to do so in years ahead.

The earliest European enterprise in the Cascades and surrounding areas was the fur trade, which began as early as 1810. Indians would trade beaver pelts to the whites in exchange for guns, blankets, knives, and other items. Surveys for a possible railroad route began in the 1860s, and these led to the earliest maps of the range. Settlers started moving into the Skykomish valley on the west and the Wenatchee valley on the east by the 1870s. Prospectors began combing every peak and valley, and it's fair to say that they went absolutely everywhere in the Cascades. The old Indian trails were improved, and by 1882 deposits at Silver Creek and Monte Cristo were discovered. Index, Galena, and Mineral City (Hike 9) grew quickly into boom towns, but more money was put into the ground in the Cascades than was ever taken out. In 1893 the Great Northern Railway was completed over the summit of Stevens Pass, a precarious route followed by a 2.6-mile tunnel seven years later and a lower, 7.8-mile tunnel completed in 1929. The Stevens Pass Highway, U.S. 2, had its beginnings with the "tote road," which was built ahead of the railroad. This was gradually improved and paved. Many of the bridges, which are now being replaced as funds permit, date from the 1930s.

Although few mining ventures ever paid, this was not the case with logging. Forests were, and are, the real wealth of the Cascades. The modern history of the Cascades is largely the history of logging, which began along Puget Sound as early as the 1850s. By 1900 a number of large sawmills were operating in Everett and logging had reached the western foothills of the Cascades.

The rapid privatization and cutting of prime forests led to the first calls for conservation and to the establishment of the national forest system in the first decade of the twentieth century. The development of small, powerful locomotives allowed railroad-based logging operations to extend into the Cascades. Lower valleys of the Beckler and the North and South Forks of the Skykomish were logged from 1920 to 1945. After World War II, the new technologies of chainsaws, bulldozers, and rubber-tired logging trucks were used to push logging deep into the Cascades. The Forest Service entered the timber business in a big way, and roads were pushed up almost all major valleys. Often, a small timber sale would be laid out at the head of a wild valley, with a road pushed through many miles of virgin forest to access it, a technique known as "wilderness preventative logging." Once the road was built, the valley would no longer be a candidate for preservation.

Many of the roadless wilderness valleys of the Cascades were lost in this way. But as more people started hiking the Cascades, many of them didn't like what they were seeing. The passage of the Wilderness Act in 1964 gave a great boost to efforts to preserve fast-shrinking wildlands and provided a new tool to protect places. The first great struggle to save a

Old cedar stump showing springboard notches of early 1900s logging techniques

wild place in the Skykomish area took place at Barclay Creek (Hike 17), where plans by the Forest Service to build a road and log several miles of old growth forest in 1966 generated spirited opposition. Although efforts to save Barclay Creek were unsuccessful, it proved to be a Pyrrhic victory for the Forest Service, since it energized a conservation movement that went on to protect large parts of the Cascades.

Barclay Creek's destruction led to intensified efforts for an Alpine Lakes Wilderness, which was finally enacted in 1976. For the first time, a large area was permanently protected in the Skykomish region, with forests in places such as Deception Creek (Hike 29) and the East Fork Foss (Hike 24) spared from planned logging. The 1984 Washington Wilderness Act focused on areas other than the Skykomish, although it did protect forests of the upper Rapid River valley.

Public awareness of the values of ancient forests grew steadily through the 1980s. A new ally for the environmental movement slowly emerged—

elements within the Forest Service itself. New blood and new ideas began to assert themselves within its ranks, and the timber beasts began to lose their grip. Forest Service planners began to appreciate the value of undisturbed forests and responded to public pressure by withdrawing plans to log in places such as the upper North Fork Skykomish (Hike 13) and West Cady Creek valleys. A forward-thinking supervisor of the Mount Baker–Snoqualmie National Forest, Doug MacWilliams, recognized that the "MBS," with millions living next to it, was an "urban forest." He made the bold move of taking the MBS out of the business of cutting old growth. The last remaining low-elevation ancient forests in the Skykomish, at Grotto, Miller River, Money Creek, and other places, thus narrowly escaped the logging that had been planned for them. Thanks in large part to him, these forests still stand, though they lack any legislative protection and may again be threatened one day.

The decline of the spotted owl was a catalyst for efforts to protect ancient forests throughout the Pacific Northwest. Lawsuits filed by environmental groups led the Clinton administration to adopt the Northwest Forest Plan in 1994, which attempted to protect not just owls but the whole range of old growth–dependent species. A system of "Late Successional Reserves" was created, and cut levels were drastically reduced. The Bush administration has started to disassemble the Northwest Forest Plan. If cut levels were to go back up, remnant old growth forests of the Skykomish region could be eliminated within a few years.

The future of the public forests in the Skykomish and adjacent country rests with concerned citizens. The Wild Sky Wilderness campaign, described in the Introduction, is the latest protection effort. "Thinning" timber sales, where only some instead of all the trees are taken from a given area, now threaten the maturing second growth forests of the lower valleys. The Forest Service makes the astonishing claim that this logging will "accelerate" the development of old growth forest. But only nature can grow an ancient forest. Thinning sales may not take every tree but they mean extensive road construction, soil compaction, and greatly increased blowdown. They leave a forest that looks very unnatural and undo decades of recovery from early logging.

The pressure from two million neighbors can lead to problems. The Cascades can accommodate pedestrians, but people with machines are another matter. Four-wheel-drive trucks are being used to push new roads and campsites into sensitive riverside areas, called, euphemistically, "dispersed recreation sites" by the Forest Service. These usually turn into squalid, muddy messes, and it remains to be seen whether the Forest Service will put a stop to them. Converting these to walk-in sites stops the damage and turns eyesores into attractions.

Virtually every conservation action, from the establishment of the national forests to the Northwest Forest Plan, has been the result of outside efforts to change the status quo. Small numbers of dedicated people have accomplished remarkable things. Not so many years ago, the Forest Service planned to cut every accessible forest in the Cascades. Determined people stopped them. Much has been accomplished, but much remains to be done. The timber industry needs to be taken entirely out of the national forests. With continued hard work, and some luck, the conservation movement in the Central Cascades may be able to make the change from just stopping bad things from happening to actually making good things happen. The authors hope that readers will contact one of the groups listed below and help out. You can make a difference.

Groups working to protect the Central Cascades:

ALPS (Alpine Lakes Protection Society)
P.O. Box 27646
Seattle, WA 98125
www.alpinelakes.org
www.wildsky.org

North Cascade Conservation Council
P.O. Box 95980
Seattle, WA 98145-1980
www.northcascades.org

Pilchuck Audubon Society
1803 Hewitt, No. 108
Everett, WA 98201
www.pilchuckaudubon.org

Sierra Club, Cascade Chapter
180 Nickerson Street, Suite 202
Seattle, WA 98109-1631
www.cascade.sierraclub.org

Washington Wilderness Coalition
4649 Sunnyside Avenue, Suite 520
Seattle, WA 98103
www.wawild.org

The Mountaineers
300 Third Avenue West
Seattle, WA 98119
(branches also in Tacoma, Everett, Olympia, Wenatchee, and Bellingham)
www.mountaineers.org

For conservation news and information specifically about the Skykomish region, see *www.wildsky.org.*

Trails: Past, Present, and Future

The Cascades need more hiking trails. The current system of trails is largely a relic of the great trailbuilding days of the 1920s and 1930s, when legendary figures such as Harold Engles and Norm McCausland located and directed the building of hundreds of miles of footpaths. After World War II the relentless expansion of logging roads wiped out much of their legacy. Today there are far fewer miles of trail in the Cascades than in 1940 but many more people interested in hiking. This has led, particularly on nice weekends in areas close to Seattle, to overcrowding on some trails—including some in this book. A growing demand for trails needs to be met. People should be able to enjoy their public lands, and trails are the best way for that to happen. Hiking has also been called the perfect low-impact aerobic exercise, just what the human body is designed for. There's no better way to keep fit. And everyone who hikes would like more choices of interesting places to do it.

At the same time, it needs to be recognized that trails have environmental costs. Some species of wildlife, such as grizzly bears and wolves, don't tolerate people well and need lots of space. A century of roadbuilding and logging has left great marks on the Cascades, and it's critical to keep development, even of trails, out of the major remaining places that are still totally undeveloped. These blank spots on the map, known more formally as core security habitat, need to be protected, both inside and outside of designated wilderness, to ensure that wildlife have undisturbed refuges. In the Cascades, the area from I-90 north has been designated as a grizzly bear recovery zone. The Forest Service and other agencies have put in place an interim set of rules designed to meet Endangered Species Act requirements by protecting core habitat there from further development. How, then, will it be possible to reconcile these two sometimes-conflicting goals of more trails and preservation of core wildlife habitat?

Fortunately, there is a way. By concentrating new trailbuilding in and near those areas that are already partially developed, the larger, undeveloped trailless areas can be mostly left alone. This approach would meet Endangered Species Act requirements. It is possible for many miles of new trails to be built to attractive destinations in such places. These would be "peripheral" trails, on the edges of trailless areas, or as longtime conservationist Harvey Manning, author of many hiking guides from The Mountaineers Books, has put it, "just outside, looking in." Additionally, people and wildlife are usually after different things in the mountains. Wildlife want food and don't care much about views. Mountainsides generally provide less food for wildlife than bottomlands, and trails that climb to viewpoints, whether on top or just on the sides of mountains, will in most cases be less disruptive to wildlife (and more attractive to people) than those that traverse low valleys and wet areas.

Hundreds of square miles of mountain terrain, with many places where new trails can be built with minimal impact on wildlife, are just east of

Seattle. Our present network of roads and trails is an accident of history and was not created with recreation or habitat protection in mind. By taking a broad landscape view, new trails can be put in the most appropriate places, getting the most bang for the buck out of scarce trail construction money. (A rough average is about $50,000 per mile to build new trails in the Cascades.) Such trails would be well suited to day hiking and, if thoughtfully laid out (such as the new Lake Serene trail, Hike 6), would be even more delightful to walk on.

The Wild Washington Campaign has put forward a draft list of new "peripheral" trail proposals as part of its campaign for the Wild Sky Wilderness.

Philadelphia Mountain: This 4258-foot-high summit stands above Lake Serene, across from Mount Index, and would make a logical extension of the new Lake Serene trail (Hike 6).

Mineral Butte: A 5255-foot-high peak with panoramic views where an old road could be converted to trail with a summit extension. See Hike 8.

Frog Mountain: Just east of main road 65 at Jack Pass, a short trail up Frog Mountain would offer broad views from huckleberry fields and a 4872-foot summit.

Excelsior Mountain: This 4832-foot summit could be reached via a side trail from the West Cady Ridge trail (Hike 11).

Evergreen Mountain: Currently reached by a precarious, failure-prone road that will be impossible to maintain over the long term, the original trail could be rebuilt from the Rapid River valley. See Hike 15.

Beckler Peak: A new trail could climb to views high above the town of Skykomish. See Hike 26.

West Fork Miller: Hike 19. Conservation groups have been working with King County to block wheels and convert this old road to trail.

Skykomish Big Trees: A classic cathedral forest of tall Douglas fir, cedar, and hemlock grows on a nearly flat bench southwest of the town of Skykomish. A short trail could reach it and a nearby viewpoint.

Some of these proposed trails would be on land partly or fully inside the boundaries of the Wild Sky Wilderness, if it is enacted. Nothing in the wilderness act prohibits trail construction. Only motorized equipment is prohibited, making trail construction potentially a bit more expensive. All Forest Service trails built before the 1970s (almost all existing trails) were built without the aid of such things as power excavators and motorized wheelbarrows, and trails can still be built that way.

1 GREIDER LAKES

Round trip: 6 miles
Hiking time: 3 hours
High point: 3600 feet
Elevation gain: 2000 feet to upper viewpoint
Hikable: June–November
Use: Light
Maps: Green Trails No. 142 Index; USGS Mount Stickney

Driving directions: Drive Highway 2 to Sultan. East of town, near the top of a hill, turn north on a road signed "Sultan Basin Recreation Area." The sign is difficult to spot when eastbound, and there is no turn lane, and traffic can be bad here. If you miss it, go farther east, turn around at some safe spot, and enter from westbound Highway 2.

Drive the Sultan Basin road, first on pavement, then gravel, to Olney Pass at 13.6 miles, the entry to the Everett watershed. Fears for the safety of the water supply have closed the watershed from time to time, but as of late 2002 it was open again. Visitors are required to register at the pass. Camping is allowed from June 15 to October 15 at Greider and Boulder Lakes only. Just beyond Olney Pass is a three-way junction. Take the middle fork 7 miles farther, passing three lake access roads on the left, to the Greider Lakes trailhead at 1550 feet, 20.7 miles from Highway 2. The land is administered by the state Department of Natural Resources, which built the trail.

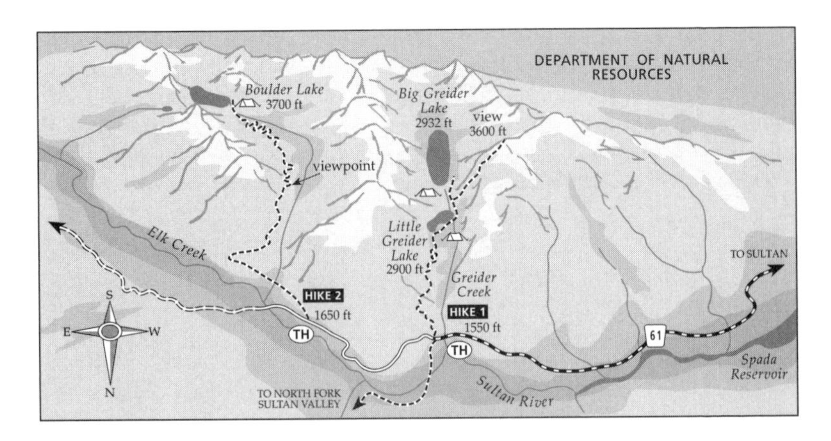

Big Greider Lake

A pleasant climb on a good trail to two scenic, cliff-ringed lakes carved out by long-vanished glaciers, and a nice viewpoint. A good late-spring hike.

The trail starts by passing a marshy area and then enters old growth forest and starts climbing numerous switchbacks. Some of the tread is rough, with boulders, roots, and a few short stairs. At 2 miles, 2900 feet, reach Little Greider Lake. The trail continues past the lake and shortly reaches scenic Big Greider Lake. For broader views, go right at a junction just before Big Greider up to a 3600-foot viewpoint, a good lunch spot looking down to the lake in its rocky cirque.

2 Boulder Lake

Round trip: 8 miles
Hiking time: 5 hours
High point: 3700 feet
Elevation gain: 2050 feet
Hikable: July–October
Use: Light
Maps: Green Trails No. 142 Index; USGS Mount Stickney

Driving directions: Drive Highway 2 to Sultan. East of town, near the top of a hill, turn north on a road signed "Sultan Basin Recreation Area." The sign is difficult to spot when eastbound, and there is no turn

Boulder Lake

lane, and traffic can be bad here. If you miss it, go farther east, turn around at some safe spot, and enter from westbound Highway 2.

Drive the Sultan Basin road, first on pavement, then gravel, to Olney Pass at 13.6 miles, the entry to the Everett watershed. The watershed has been closed at times for security reasons, but as of late 2002 it was open again. Visitors are required to register at the pass. Camping is allowed from June 15 to October 15 at Greider and Boulder Lakes only. Just beyond Olney Pass is a three-way junction. Take the middle fork 7 miles farther, passing three lake access roads on the left, to the Greider Lakes trailhead at 20.7 miles from Highway 2. Just past the Greider Lakes trailhead turn right at a road junction and follow this road 1.2 miles farther to the Boulder Lake trailhead, elevation 1650 feet.

A surprisingly beautiful and little-visited lake on state DNR land.

The trail starts on an eroding old logging road that turns to trail and crosses a brushy, rocky area, reaching a viewpoint at 1½ miles. From here the trail is a real joy as it winds up through old growth on a secluded track. At about 3 miles, some marshy spots are traversed on puncheons and the trail switchbacks up a headwall, shortly reaching Boulder Lake. The outlet area has a nice mix of forest and meadow and a great view. The lake itself is a pleasing azure color. The "boulders" are at the far end of the lake and often snow covered through July. There are campsites, and the mystery of why more people don't come to enjoy this place.

3 North Fork Sultan Valley

Round trip: 12 miles
Hiking time: 6–8 hours
High point: 2200 feet
Elevation gain: 700 feet
Hikable: August–October
Use: Light
Maps: Green Trails No. 142 Index; USGS Mount Stickney, Monte Cristo

Driving directions: Drive Highway 2 to Sultan. East of town, near the top of a hill, turn north on a road signed "Sultan Basin Recreation Area." The sign is difficult to spot when eastbound, and there is no turn lane, and traffic can be bad here. If you miss it, go farther east, turn around at some safe spot, and enter from westbound Highway 2.

Drive the Sultan Basin road, first on pavement, then gravel, to Olney Pass at 13.6 miles, the entry to the Everett watershed. The watershed has been closed at times for security reasons, but as of late 2002 it was open again. Visitors are required to register at the pass. Camping is allowed from June 15 to October 15 at Greider and Boulder Lakes only. Just beyond Olney Pass is a three-way junction. Take the middle fork 7 miles farther, passing three lake access roads on the left, to the Greider Lakes trailhead at 1550 feet and park here, 20.7 miles from Highway 2.

An old mining road follows the North Fork Sultan River into this spectacular, little-known valley below massive peaks. The North Fork valley largely escaped the 1960–1990 logging, which devastated most of the Sultan Basin country. Most of the valley is state DNR land, with the uppermost mile in national forest and proposed for protection in the Wild Sky Wilderness. A river ford near the beginning is potentially tricky and should be attempted only during low water. The City of Everett allows only day use here.

From the Greider Lakes trailhead, walk down an old road, which drops to the left at a junction next to the trailhead. Go past a collapsed bridge and follow the river a short distance upstream. Pass an old cabin and descend to the rocky banks of the river. Scout out a safe crossing if the river is low enough.

On the other side, the nearly level road follows the river closely north, then east into the North Fork valley. At 3 miles pass a very 1960s-style, "gee-whiz"–type watershed sign, placed here long ago by the state DNR when the road was drivable and the watershed was being scalped. At 4 miles an old brushy road takes off left and climbs to several old mines and

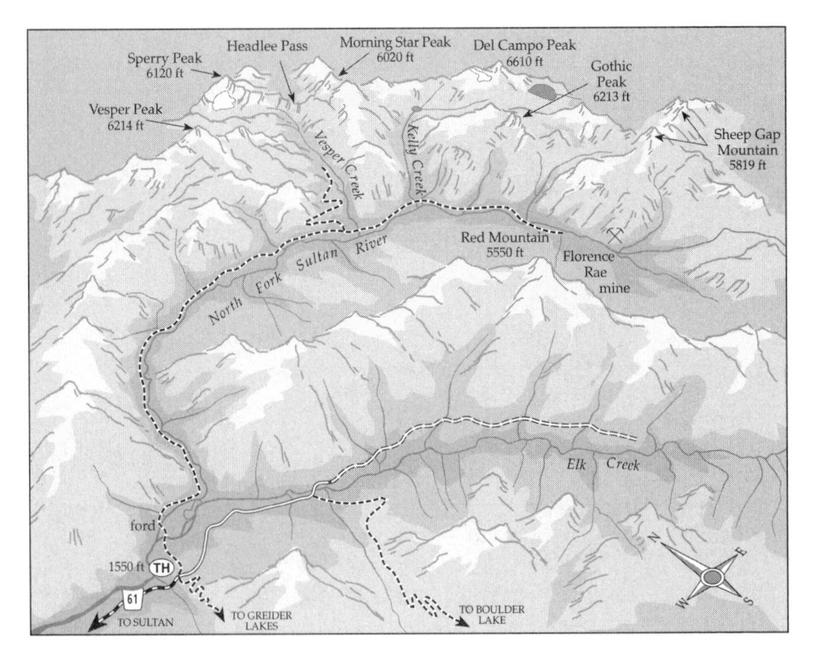

a long-abandoned trail, which eventually joins the maintained Forest Service Sunrise Mine trail near Headlee Pass far above.

Continue straight ahead and cross Vesper Creek on an old bridge, which may be gone by the time you get there. Pass the remains of a cabin and an active beaver pond, and cross several more decaying bridges. At 5½ miles a side road goes right to the semidry riverbed. Just past it is an old DNR picnic grounds, laid out years ago and now a curious relic from another era. Continue ahead and cross yet another deteriorating but photogenic bridge. Pass under a cable, the remnant of an old mine tramway. A cabin in a clearing comes into view, a good destination from which to look north to the tremendous rocky bulk of Gothic Peak and west to the fearsomely steep and brushy slopes of Red Mountain. It's easy to see why Red has seldom been climbed. Adventurous souls can try to find a faint brushy trail that climbs another thousand vertical feet or so to the remains of the Florence Rae mine.

Upper North Fork Sultan valley from Crested Butte; Red Mountain on the left, Vesper Peak to the right Photo by John Roper

Wallace Falls

Round trip: 5–6 miles
Hiking time: 2–3 hours
High point: 1600 feet
Elevation gain: 1250 feet
Hikable: All year
Use: Heavy
Maps: Green Trails No. 142 Index; USGS Gold Bar, Wallace Lake

Driving directions: Drive Highway 2 to Gold Bar, where signs point the way to the state park with its rather small parking area (elevation 350 feet), which can fill up on nice weekends. At present there is no overflow parking area, and "No Parking" signs line the road below the park entrance. Parking outside the gate means risking a ticket. If the lot is full, consider hiking elsewhere or parking in Gold Bar and walking the mile to the park.

Only the most jaded driver could ignore the sight of Wallace Falls from Highway 2 north of Gold Bar. This miniature Niagara sits amid dense second growth forest below Mount Stickney. Not so long ago it was a

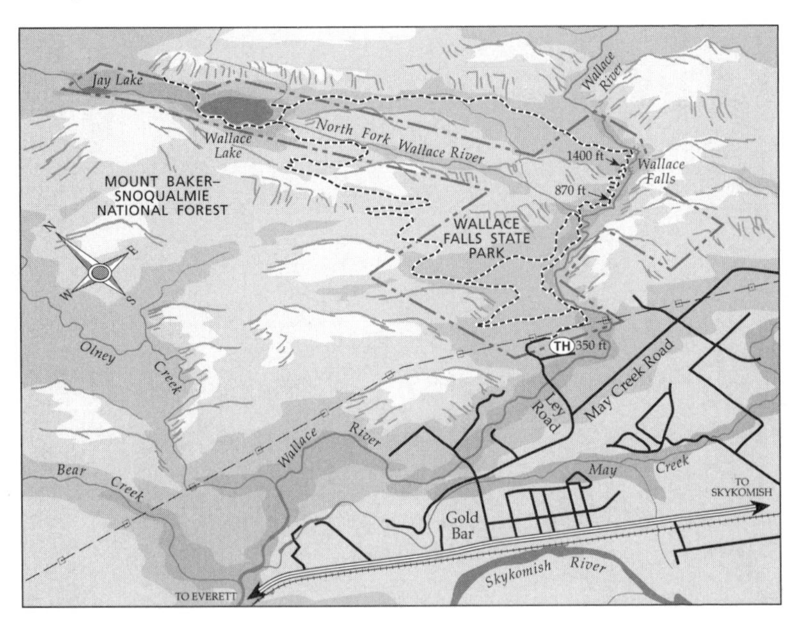

Wallace Falls

routefinding challenge along a confusing array of old logging grades, but Wallace Falls State Park has opened it to the masses, and it is now one of the most popular walks along the Stevens Pass Highway, deservedly so. It's one of the few trails that are dependably snowfree year 'round—if there's snow here, there's snow in Seattle, too. For maximum drama, go during snowmelt time in spring.

The trail follows powerlines a short distance and then plunges into the forest to a junction. The left route follows gentle railroad grades 2 miles; the right route goes a steeper 1 mile near the river to where the trails rejoin. Veterans recommend the river route up and the railroad grade down. From the upper junction, the trail crosses the North Fork Wallace (not the fork from the falls) and climbs ¼ mile to a picnic shelter (870 feet) with the first view of the falls. Keep on to a middle viewpoint (probably the best) at 1120 feet. At 2½ miles the trail passes a few older trees and reaches the top of the first falls (the one seen from the highway) at 1400 feet, with views down to the valley below. The misty gorge is a sight to behold, especially during high water, when the ground seems to vibrate. A steep half-mile or so of trail climbs beyond here to views of the more enclosed upper falls. Take care to stay behind the railings; there have been several fatal slips here.

From the lower railroad grade, a side route follows old grades and newer roads for a long 6 miles, crossing some clearcuts, to Wallace Lake (the lake itself, though not its environs, is part of the park). From here, possible routes lead to little Jay Lake and up toward Mount Stickney. Sadly, the state park is not big enough to encompass much of the surrounding lands, and new roads on state DNR and private lands are punching through what was until recently a delightful second growth wilderness. The view from Highway 2 (though not from the falls themselves) is fast deteriorating and will likely soon be of a dramatic waterfall with clearcuts encroaching on all sides.

5 Lake Isabel

Round trip: 6 miles
Hiking time: 5–6 hours
High point: 2842 feet
Elevation gain: 2300 feet
Hikable: May–November
Use: Light (heavy ORV use in lower areas)
Maps: Green Trails No. 142 Index (trail not shown); USGS Gold Bar, Index (trail shown)

Driving directions: Drive Highway 2 some 2 miles east of Gold Bar to turn north on Reiter Road, just opposite milepost 30. At 2 miles pass an abandoned gravel pit, cross a bridge, and turn left on a DNR logging road. At 0.4 mile go left at a junction onto a terribly potholed road. Half a mile from the junction, reach May Creek and the end of the passable road.

A tremendous waterfall, views, and one of the largest mountain lakes in the Cascades. Unfortunately, the way starts out through the worst ORV hell in the Skykomish valley. Perhaps someday the state DNR will put a

Lake Isabel

stop to the horrendous damage being done by motorcycles, quads, and Jeeps, and a decent foot trail will be built. For now, plan to go on a weekday when the motorheads are less numerous.

The bridge over May Creek is long gone. Boulder-hop or wade across, find the road on the other side, and hike away from the creek, reaching a

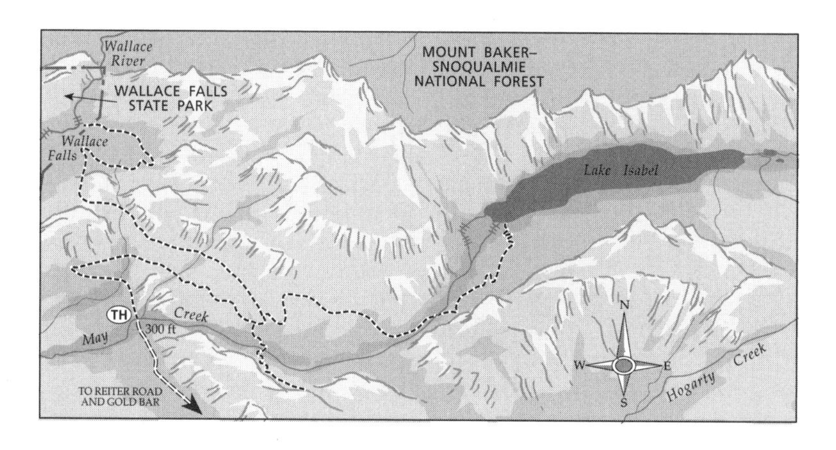

switchback at ¾ mile. Turn right, and at just under 2 miles reach a second switchback and junction. Turn left and shortly reach yet another switchback and junction. Turn right, climb, and follow the road another 1 mile to where it crosses May Creek on a very old bridge. Cross the creek and climb upward on the steep rocky road, avoiding a path that leads straight at a curve in the road. Just under ½ mile from the bridge, spot the inconspicuous path to Lake Isabel taking off to the left. About 200 yards beyond the path the road reaches a viewpoint worth going to.

The trail enters old growth forest soon after leaving the road, passing some nice cedars. Reach the impressive outlet falls in ½ mile; the trail climbs steeply and precariously up to the right of it. Note the hundreds of small yew trees growing in the mist from the falls. Suddenly the top is reached, and the long expanse of Lake Isabel, 176 acres, 200 feet deep in spots.

Steep, brushy shores make it virtually impossible to hike along the lake, and there's nowhere farther to go. An inflatable raft is the only practicable way to reach and fish the upper end ("mackinaw" trout have reportedly reached 30 inches here). However, the lake is famous for turning from glassy smooth into an ocean within minutes, especially in the afternoon when sudden winds kick up. The unfriendly shores offer few escape routes.

The lake has also become a test of bravado with floatplane fliers, some of whom have paid for slight miscalculations with their lives. At least two floatplanes are on the bottom of the lake, and a botched takeoff a few years ago killed several in a fiery collision with the mountainside. The air approach to the lake is strictly one way; once past a certain point, there's no turning back or trying again. The lake will become part of the Wild Sky Wilderness if enacted, but floatplane use will continue unless stopped by separate Forest Service action.

Recent logging may make finding the Lake Isabel trail even more complicated. Should this happen, try to follow newer roads to rejoin the route described here near its upper crossing of May Creek.

Waterfalls on May Creek, below Lake Isabel

6 Lake Serene

Round trip: 8 miles
Hiking time: 4–5 hours
High point: 2550 feet
Elevation gain: 2000 feet
Hikable: June–November
Use: Heavy
Maps: Green Trails No. 142 Index; USGS Index (trail too new to appear on maps)

Driving directions: Drive Highway 2 to milepost 35, east of Gold Bar. Just before the highway crosses the Skykomish on a big old bridge, turn right (south) onto the gravel "Mt. Index" road, go 0.3 mile, and take the first right, to a large parking area.

If one had to pick the absolute scenic high point of the entire Highway 2 corridor, it would have to be Mount Index. A few miles east of Gold Bar, the highway rounds a corner, and it hits you right in the face. It's amazing that there aren't more accidents here. Another mile and the whole mountain is revealed, from the upper walls to the white ribbon of Bridal Veil Falls. Tucked improbably amid the cliffs is Lake Serene.

The original "trail" was a dangerous ladder of roots and mud, and side paths to the falls claimed a few lives over the years. But the Forest Service has now completed a beautiful new trail, thoughtfully designed and laid out. Future trail planners would do well to study the efforts that went into it. The spirit of Harold Engles, legendary ranger and most famous trail-builder of the Cascades, lives on in today's Forest Service.

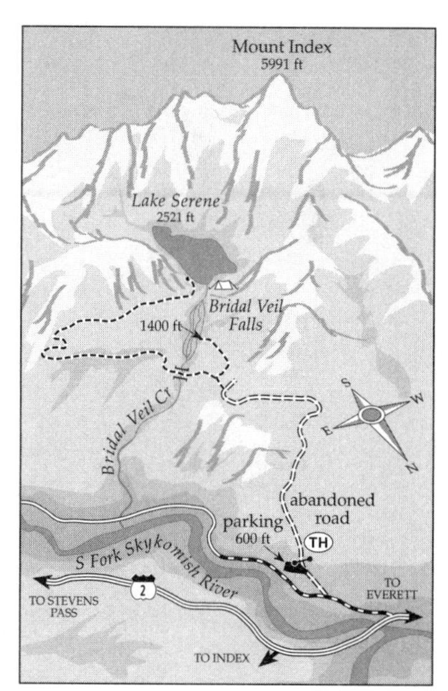

The trail starts out on an old road through forest on land that may be logged at some point. (If this happens, the trail will likely be closed during logging but should reopen soon after.) In 1¾ miles a junction is reached. Go right ½ mile for a mist-and-spray view of Bridal

Veil Falls, straight ahead for Lake Serene. A sturdy bridge crosses Bridal Veil Creek and the trail passes almost underneath a side falls just after. Then it starts upward, entering a respectable forest of big spruces, hemlocks, and Douglas fir. Keeping to a good stiff grade it climbs, partly on stairs, over and under cliffs, with glimpses north toward Ragged Ridge, Gunn Peak, and Mount Baring, and down to the Index Town Wall. After a long but pleasant 2 miles from the junction, the trail swings into the hanging basin of Lake Serene, elevation 2521 feet.

Seeing is believing. The clear lake sits right below the fearsome, dark,

Lake Serene and Mount Index

2000-foot east walls of Mount Index. Warm days early in the season send lots of snow and rock cannonading down toward the lake, and the show can be safely watched (and heard) from near the outlet. Cliffs and brushy shores limit further explorations, but who could ask for anything more?

There may, however, be more one day. Conservation groups have proposed extending the trail from Lake Serene on up to the 4258-foot top of Philadelphia Mountain, about 1½ miles to the southeast, for high-level views to the North Fork Sky country and across to the walls of Index. As of now, the way is brushy and not recommended, but "watch this space."

7 TROUT CREEK AND IRON MOUNTAIN

Round trip to Trout Creek: 8 miles
Hiking time: 4–5 hours
High point: 2200 feet
Elevation gain: 1400 feet
Hikable: April–November
Use: Light

Round trip to Iron Mountain: 7 miles
Hiking time: 4–5 hours
High point: 3400 feet
Elevation gain: 2600 feet
Hikable: June–October
Use: Light

Maps: Green Trails No. 143 Monte Cristo (roads not shown); USGS Baring (roads shown)

Driving directions: Drive Highway 2 to the Index turnoff, then turn north on the Index–Galena road. This road changes its name along the way—the lower, county-maintained part is the Index–Galena road, while the upper part is the North Fork road. Go past the town of Index to a road just past the bridge over Trout Creek, 6.2 miles from the highway. Turn right on the road and almost immediately park in a clearing, elevation 800 feet.

This quiet valley cuts into the proposed Sky Peaks unit of the proposed Wild Sky Wilderness. The Trout Creek option goes past the Sunset Mine along an old logging grade, while the Iron Mountain route climbs an old road to some views across the valley toward Gunn Peak.

At the clearing where you parked, ignore the side road dropping to the

Hiker on the Iron Mountain road, overlooking Trout Creek

creek and begin hiking up the road past an old gate. The road sweeps uphill, becoming very rough. A few jeeps and other four-wheel-drives still go up it, but this requires a driver willing to clash steel on rock, and as the road gets worse every year the drivers grow fewer. Hopefully it will soon be entirely wheelfree. At ¾ mile a junction is reached: Iron Mountain is up and to the left, Trout Creek is straight ahead. At 1½ miles on the lower road the ruins of the Sunset Mine are reached. Little remains now but rubble, all the interesting relics having been carted away long ago. There's not much to indicate that this was just about the most productive and profitable mine

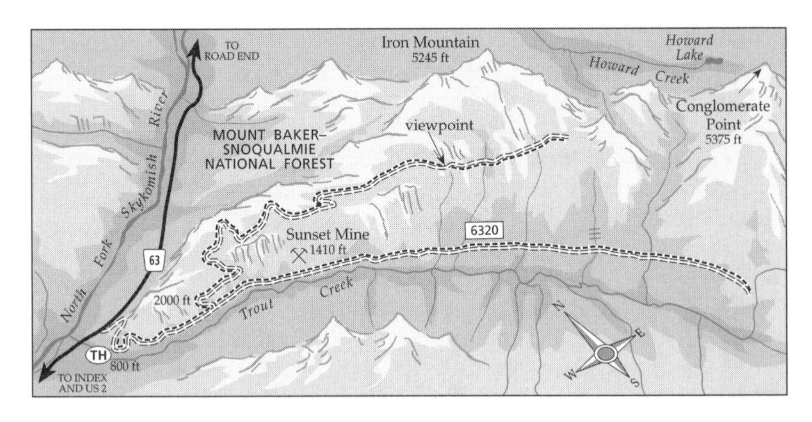

ever to operate in the Cascades. From 1926 to 1945, its 12,000 feet of underground tunnels yielded 13 million pounds of copper and 150,000 ounces of silver, surpassing the combined output of all the mines at Monte Cristo.

Beyond the mine, follow the old road for another 2 to 2½ miles through pleasant second growth forest. About a mile beyond the mine a band of old growth forest is traversed, and not far beyond is a picturesque little stairstep waterfall right along the road. The way grows gradually brushier as the road disappears into the young forest.

For the Iron Mountain route, go left at the junction at ¾ mile, and then follow the old road relentlessly up through second growth woods. At one switchback at the 2000-foot level, pause to see a large tracked excavator that didn't quite make the turn and tumbled over the edge into the forest. It must have been quite a sight, and one wonders about the fate of the operator. At about 3½ miles a granite rib is passed, offering views over Trout Creek valley to Gunn Peak and Jumpoff Ridge. Trees are slowly obscuring the views, both here and farther up the road, which starts to get brushy and climbs another mile or so to its end in a reforesting clearcut.

8 Mineral Butte

Round trip: 12 miles
Hiking time: 5–7 hours
High point: 5255 feet
Elevation gain: 3700 feet
Hikable: July–October (possible to snowshoe/ski here in winter)
Use: Light
Maps: Green Trails No. 142 Index, No. 143 Monte Cristo (road not shown); USGS Monte Cristo

Driving directions: Take the Index turnoff from Highway 2 and follow the Index–Galena road (also known as the North Fork road) a bit more than 9 miles north, where just past Howard Creek a road to the left crosses the North Fork on a concrete bridge. Cross the bridge, go straight at the junction just past the bridge, and continue 1.4 miles to park at the first switchback.

An eroding logging road climbs high on the southeast ridge of Mineral Butte, with a sketchy trail beyond through huckleberry meadows to expansive views. The relatively gentle high terrain is good for winter snowshoeing or skiing with little avalanche danger except near the very top. The Wild Washington Campaign has proposed converting the road into a foot trail, with an extension to the summit.

Hiker on Mineral Butte

From where most people will park, it is possible to drive farther, but the road quickly gets rough, then very rough, then extremely rough. Occasional pieces of vehicles attest to the few drivers with more guts than brains who still attempt it. If ever there was a road in desperate need of decommissioning, this is it.

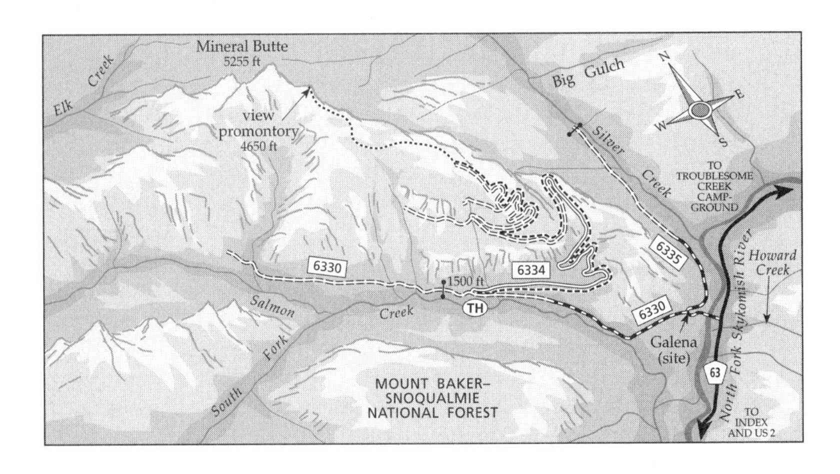

Follow the road, passing several junctions, always keeping to the "main" road, which gains the most elevation. The road climbs and climbs through clearcuts, seemingly without end, but views grow better with every step. After passing through a remnant band of old growth, the road finally does end in a clearcut at about the 4000-foot level. This expensive and now crumbling road was built in the 1970s by the Forest Service to access poor timber barely worth cutting even when practically given away. It will take this forest many centuries to recover.

Above the road's end, head northwest and find an ORV-carved path in the forest. Fortunately, few ORVs make it up this far, but this trail shows the kind of damage that just a few of these machines can do to high meadow country. Conservationists have for years been asking the Forest Service to stop them by blocking the road at a low-elevation chokepoint, but nothing has ever been done. Follow the "trail" up through the woods, soon breaking into really delightful huckleberry and heather meadows interspersed with mountain hemlock forest. Some flattish open areas are crossed, and a few gentle ridges, good ski and snowshoe terrain. About 1½ miles from the road, the "trail" ends near a rock promontory at 4650 feet, 5½ miles from the parking spot, with stunning views north up the Silver Creek valley toward the Monte Cristo peaks and southeast to Spire Peak.

The rock outcrop is a logical destination for most hikers, but it is possible to continue climbing northwest, scrambling through forest and up a field of sometimes tippy boulders to the 5255-foot summit of Mineral Butte. Panoramic 360-degree views take in the entire North Fork, Monte Cristo, and upper Sultan areas. If a real trail were built here, it would soon be one of the most popular destinations in the whole Skykomish country.

SILVER CREEK–MINERAL CITY

Round trip: 7 miles
Hiking time: 4–5 hours
High point: 2200 feet
Elevation gain: 800 feet
Hikable: May–November
Use: Light
Maps: Green Trails No. 143 Monte Cristo; USGS Monte Cristo

Driving directions: Follow Highway 2 to the Index turnoff. Go just over 9 miles up the Index–Galena road (also known as the North Fork road) and just past the Howard Creek bridge take a left on Forest Service road 6330. Cross the North Fork Skykomish on a concrete bridge, and after a few hundred feet turn right on Silver Creek road 6335. High-clearance vehicles can usually drive 1.5 miles; others will want to stop sooner where the road is rough. A deep wash stops most wheels 600 feet from a barricade at elevation 1400 feet.

Follow an old mining road along the original route to Monte Cristo, past an amazing, deep rock gorge to the site of Mineral City, which once boasted two hotels, several bars, and other enterprises. Nothing remains of it today, no minerals, no city—it is so thoroughly erased that most of the valley is proposed to be part of the Wild Sky Wilderness.

The old mining road was widened into a logging road in the 1970s, which led to its dramatic collapse. Hundreds of feet of mountainside went with it, and it remains the most damaging and sediment-bleeding road failure in the North Fork watershed. Nothing has been done to stabilize it. The trail across the slide is airy but not difficult and rejoins the old roadbed a short ways north. The road passes a couple of drippy mine openings and crosses a couple of sagging wooden bridges spanning steep side canyons. These bridges will likely not survive many more winters, and crossing the side canyons would be difficult and dangerous without them, so go soon.

The road passes above the deep slot gorge of Silver Creek, where smooth rock walls plunge down to green, inaccessible pools. Several side streams pour off overhangs and fall free into the pools. This gorge is one of the beauty spots of the Skykomish country, but it took a beating from a 1989 timber sale. Despite repeated assurances that the gorge itself would be spared, trees were cut right in the heart of it, an act of pure vandalism by the Forest Service. Most fell uselessly into the gorge, though a few were helicoptered out after the destruction made it onto TV newscasts. Floods have now swept the gorge clean, and the scars are beginning to heal.

The gorge itself makes a splendid short walk. Above it, the valley opens up, the road paralleling Silver Creek through a mix of old and young forest. At 3½ miles is the site of Mineral City. Fires and floods obliterated it

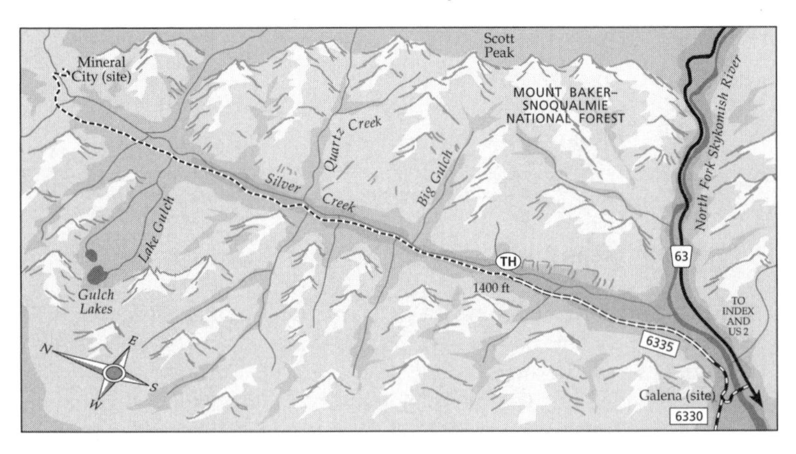

Old mine in the Silver Creek valley

decades ago, and the forest is reclaiming its own. An open area along the unnamed creek, which joins Silver Creek from the west, provides views. The road crosses Silver Creek on a still-solid wooden bridge and then climbs east and north to its end. The aptly named slash of Red Gulch can be seen across to the west. Alders are rapidly reforesting the road-end landing but a few view windows still make good lunch and turnaround spots. Bits of the old trail beyond to Poodle Dog Pass and Monte Cristo can be found, but as of 2003 there was more brush than trail, not recommended for any but dedicated masochists.

10 BLANCA LAKE

Round trip: 8 miles
Hiking time: 4–6 hours
High point: 4600 feet
Elevation gain: 2700 feet in, 600 feet out
Hikable: June–October
Use: Heavy
Maps: Green Trails No. 143 Monte Cristo; USGS Blanca Lake

Driving directions: Take the Index turnoff from Highway 2 and follow the Index–Galena road (also known as the North Fork road) north for

Blanca Lake

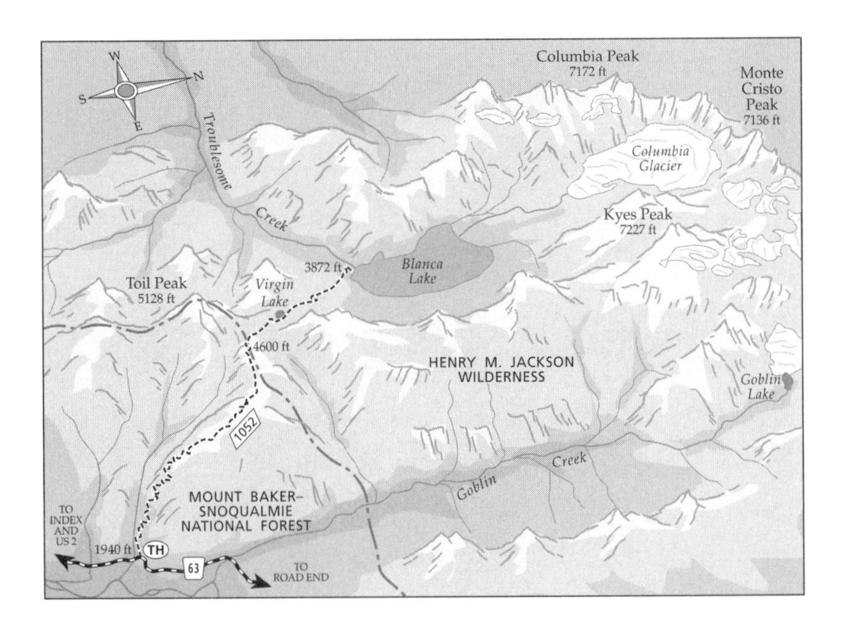
W
N
S
E
Columbia Peak
7172 ft
Monte
Cristo
Peak
7136 ft
Troublesome
Creek
Columbia
Glacier
Kyes Peak
7227 ft
3872 ft
Blanca
Lake
Toil Peak
5128 ft
Virgin
Lake
4600 ft
HENRY M. JACKSON
WILDERNESS
Goblin
Lake
1052
Creek
Goblin
MOUNT BAKER–
SNOQUALMIE
NATIONAL FOREST
TO
INDEX
AND
US 2
1940 ft
TH
63
TO
ROAD END

14.8 miles to a four-way junction, where the pavement ends. Turn left and follow road 63 for 2 miles to the trailhead.

Azure-colored Blanca Lake sits in a large, glacier-scooped rock bowl beneath the shrinking but still considerable Columbia Glacier, which is ringed by the cliffs of Columbia, Monte Cristo, and Kyes Peaks. The glacier is responsible for the lake's color, tinting Troublesome Creek and even the North Fork Skykomish down as far as Index. But the lake is only one of the attractions here, which include a slope of unbroken old growth forest and a high ridge with a small lake sitting improbably atop it.

The trail climbs gentle but numerous switchbacks through a very attractive forest of old growth Douglas fir, gradually changing to silver fir and mountain hemlock as the 2700 feet to the ridge top are gained. This is a good place to look for calypso orchids and other forest flowers in June. The path tops out and swings past Virgin Lake and some meadows with views to the east, then deteriorates and plunges 600 feet downhill to the outlet of Blanca Lake, quite a spot. It's possible to cross the outlet and find some campsites, but the ridge top offers better exploring and wider views.

11 West Cady Ridge–Bench Mark Mountain

Round trip to viewpoint: 8 miles
Hiking time: 4 hours
High point: 4761 feet
Elevation gain: 2200 feet
Hikable: June–October
Use: Moderate

Round trip to Bench Mark Mountain: 16 miles
Hiking time: 9 hours
High point: 5816 feet
Elevation gain: 3300 feet
Hikable: June–October
Use: Moderate

Maps: Green Trails No. 143 Monte Cristo, No. 144 Bench Mark Mtn.; USGS Blanca Lake, Bench Mark Mtn.

Driving directions: Drive Highway 2 to the Index turnoff. Turn north and drive 14.8 miles up the Index–Galena road (also known as the North Fork road) to a four-way junction, where the pavement ends. Turn left on road 63 and follow it 4.5 miles to the trailhead for West

Cady Ridge and Quartz Creek, and hopefully soon for the North Fork Skykomish as well.

This hike has it all—a cool ascent through shady old growth forest, miles of ridge top meadows, and views, views, and views. The trail is in good shape thanks to volunteer maintenance by the Cascade Chapter of the Sierra Club. It's a bit of a workout, though; be sure to carry plenty of water.

The route starts on the south side of the road and soon crosses the North Fork on a high wooden bridge. It then climbs well-graded switchbacks through a very impressive forest of Douglas fir, hemlock, and cedar, which last saw a fire in about the year 1308, making the large Douglas fir trees 700 years old. A saddle between West Cady and Excelsior Mountain is reached, and then another climb through younger forest tops out on West Cady Ridge and the start of delightful meadow country. Four miles from the start, a 4761-foot high point has views north toward the Monte Cristo peaks and Glacier Peak, west to the Sky Peaks area, and south across the forested valley of West Cady Creek.

For Bench Mark Mountain, follow the trail east from here 4 more miles

West Cady Ridge, Columbia and Kyes Peaks in the distance

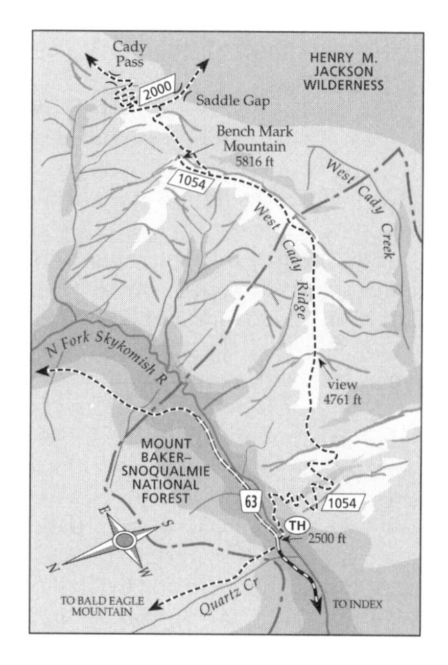

through flowers and berry fields to the summit and endless views. The great sweep of virgin forest in the North Fork Skykomish valley is a particularly appealing, and all too rare, sight. A lookout cabin once stood here, and the mountain narrowly escaped having a road blasted to the summit as part of a "scenic parkway" scheme, which fortunately never came to pass. Early season might provide some snowmelt but for most of the summer there is no water, so plan accordingly. A fire burned the ridge in 1918, and berry-rich bear habitat stretches for miles; this would not be a good place to bring your dog. If you get tired of the mountain views, try scanning the meadow country for bears. The chances of spotting one are good, especially early and late in the day. It's possible to loop back to the car by descending the Pass Creek trail (Hike 14) to the North Fork trail and walking 1.3 miles of road that hopefully will become part of the Wild Sky Wilderness and be converted to trail someday soon.

12 Quartz Creek–Curry Gap–Bald Eagle Trail

Round trip: 13 miles
Hiking time: 6–7 hours
High point: 5200 feet
Elevation gain: 2700 feet
Hikable: June–October
Use: Moderate
Maps: Green Trails No. 143 Monte Cristo, No. 144 Bench Mark Mtn.; USGS Blanca Lake, Bench Mark Mtn.

Driving directions: Drive Highway 2 to the Index turnoff. Turn north and drive 14.8 miles up the Index–Galena road (also known as the North Fork road) to a four-way junction, where the pavement ends. Turn left on road 63 and follow it 4.5 miles to the trailhead for West Cady

Ridge and Quartz Creek, and hopefully soon for the North Fork Skykomish as well.

A nice day hike through ancient forests of Quartz Creek to a high ridge trail with views and flowers. Beyond the scope of this book are miles of subalpine wandering on trails where you'll meet more marmots than people.

From the parking area, head north on the Quartz Creek trail, which climbs gently through 4½ miles of very old forest to the narrow defile of Curry Gap. Look for queen's cup, pipsissewa, coral root, and the ghostly Indian pipe. Give thanks that the Forest Service road engineers ran out of money before they could build another "scenic" road up this valley to connect with roads coming south from Darrington.

Several tumbling creeks are crossed, and views into Goblin Basin to the west begin to open up approaching Curry Gap. From the Gap, the trail straight ahead descends 3½ miles to the Sloan Creek road. Take the right fork, which switchbacks up to the east with expanding views. Beyond Curry Gap 1½ miles, the trail reaches the 5200-foot ridge, a good day hike lunch spot with views west to Kyes, Monte Cristo, and Cadet Peaks.

For backpackers, the trail continues for miles, contouring the side of Bald Eagle Mountain, with changing views as the trail continues east on or

Monte Cristo Peaks from Bald Eagle Mountain trail

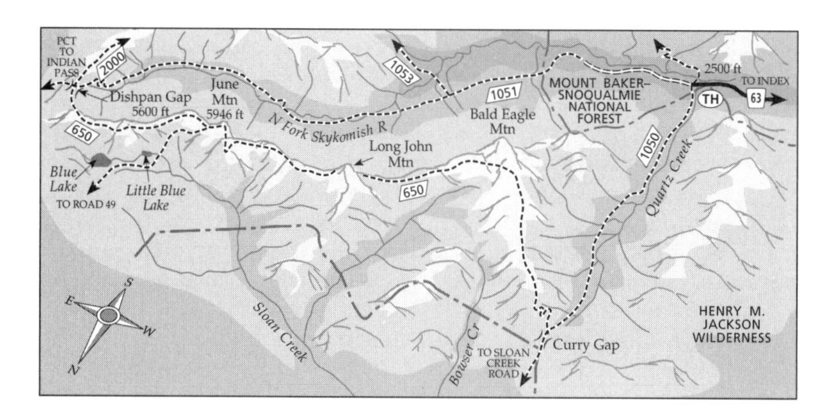

near the Skykomish–Sauk divide to Long John Mountain and June Mountain, eventually reaching Dishpan Gap and the North Fork Sky trail (Hike 13). Connections north are also possible, offering days of wandering.

13 North Fork Skykomish–Dishpan Gap

Round trip to river ford: 8 miles
Hiking time: 3–4 hours
High point: 3700 feet
Elevation gain: 700 feet
Hikable: June–October
Use: Moderate

Round trip to Dishpan Gap: 15 miles
Hiking time: 6–8 hours
High point: 5600 feet
Elevation gain: 2600 feet
Hikable: July–October
Use: Moderate

Maps: Green Trails No. 144 Bench Mark Mtn.; USGS Bench Mark Mtn.

Driving directions: Drive Highway 2 to the Index turnoff. Turn north and drive 14.8 miles up the Index–Galena road (also known as the North Fork road) to a four-way junction, where the pavement ends. Turn left on road 63 and follow it 4.5 miles to the trailhead for West Cady Ridge and Quartz Creek, and hopefully soon for the North Fork Skykomish as well.

Other than along a short road corridor, no logging has been done in the upper North Fork valley, and the vista of its unbroken old growth forests is a dramatic sight. During the 1960s, plans were laid for yet another "scenic" road that would have gone up the North Fork and Pass Creek (Hike 13) and over Cady Pass to Lake Wenatchee. Fortunately, sanity prevailed and only the first 1.3 miles of the road were punched through this otherwise untouched valley.

East of the parking area, the 1.3 miles of "scenic" road beyond were still passable to high-clearance vehicles in 2003. The mileages here are from the end of the 1.3 miles, but if you don't want to risk your car, park at the West Cady trailhead and walk the deteriorating but pleasant road. The Forest Service promised to close this 1.3 miles in 1989 and convert it to trail, thus allowing for two grand trail loops without the need for any road walking. The current Skykomish district ranger has chosen not to implement the conversion, but if the Wild Sky Wilderness is enacted, the valley here will be part of it. This will permanently protect the forest and require the Forest Service to carry out its commitment of more than a decade ago.

The old road traverses superb old growth forest, with some especially nice big corky-barked Douglas firs believed to be up to 700 years old. At the road's end the trail immediately plunges into the forest. Following a

North Fork Skykomish River trail

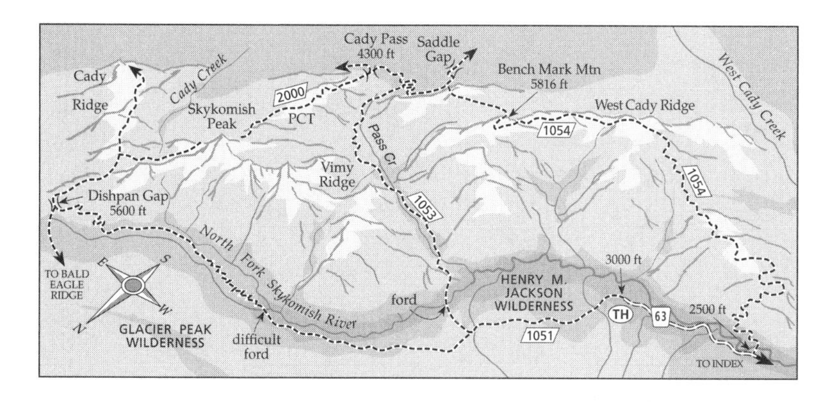

gentle grade, more monster trees are passed. At 1½ miles from the road's end, a junction with the Pass Creek trail (Hike 14) is reached. Continue straight, and mostly level, through more forest until at 3½ miles the trail crosses the unbridged river. Late in the year it's usually possible to boulder-hop across; otherwise it's a wade. Early in the season the river level makes this a good turnaround spot.

If there is still energy and a hunger for views and flowers, the trail can be followed to Dishpan Gap. Across the river the trail ascends an interesting low ridge, which separates the North Fork and a creek to the south that parallels it for nearly a mile. A gorgeous semiforested meadow is then reached, with acres of waist-high huckleberry bushes. After another mile, the trail switchbacks up the valley headwall to an alpine meadow, then makes the final climb to Dishpan Gap.

From Dishpan Gap one trail leads northwest to Bald Eagle Ridge (Hike 12) and the Pacific Crest Trail heads south to Cady Pass (Hike 14), both very worthwhile loops. The Crest Trail north goes to many miles of further exploration possibilities. A 5892-foot hill just north of Dishpan Gap provides expansive views of Glacier Peak and down into the headwaters of the Skykomish, Sauk, and Little Wenatchee valleys.

Devil's club

14 Pass Creek–Cady Pass

Round trip: 10⅗ miles
Hiking time: 4–6 hours
High point: 4300 feet
Elevation gain: 1300 feet
Hikable: June–October
Use: Moderate
Maps: Green Trails No. 144 Bench Mark Mtn.; USGS Bench Mark Mtn.

Driving directions: Drive Highway 2 to the Index turnoff. Turn north and drive 14.8 miles up the Index–Galena road (also known as the North Fork road) to a four-way junction, where the pavement ends. Turn left on road 63 and follow it 4.5 miles to the trailhead for West Cady Ridge and Quartz Creek, and hopefully soon for the North Fork Skykomish as well.

Follow a route used for many centuries by Native Americans to cross the Cascades. Old growth forests and an unusual low-elevation meadow add interest, and two loop trips are possible.

From the trailhead, another 1.3 miles of decaying but pleasant road continue east. If you don't want to risk your car's undercarriage, park at the

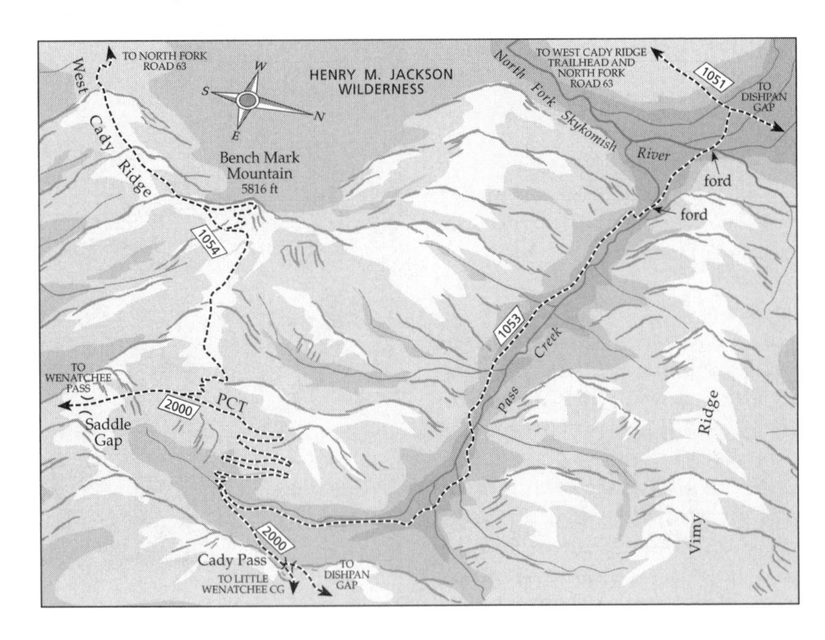

West Cady trailhead and enjoy the walk and the old growth forest. At road's end the trail plunges into yet more splendid forest. Follow it 1½ miles to a junction and turn right on the Pass Creek trail. Descend and find a way across the North Fork Skykomish; usually there is a footlog or logjam and wading is not difficult except during high run-off. Just after the river the trail crosses a boggy meadow area on boardwalk. Here the small, carnivorous sundew plant can be found. Look for a red leaf the size of a dime surrounded by sticky globules. Flies caught in the globules are rolled up by the leaves and digested.

The trail leaves the wet meadows and re-enters the old forest, which has not seen a fire since 1308. Pass Creek is reached at 2¼ miles. Cross the

The Pass Creek trail in old growth forest

unbridged creek and follow the trail through forest of hemlock and silver fir to a junction with the Pacific Crest Trail at 5 miles. The trail left reaches forested Cady Pass in ¼ mile, and a loop hike is possible if one heads north to Dishpan Gap and returns down the North Fork valley (Hike 13). Another option is to turn right at the Pacific Crest Trail junction and take another right in less than a mile to climb Bench Mark Mountain from the east and return via West Cady Ridge (Hike 11).

Cady Pass was a main Indian trade and travel route. In 1838 a smallpox epidemic killed many of the Skykomish people and the trail was little used until it was reopened by Ed Cady, a founder of Snohomish, in 1859. Cady Pass was the major route across this part of the Cascades until Stevens Pass was opened up by the Great Northern Railway in 1893. A scheme by the Forest Service to build a "scenic parkway" over Cady Pass, with a spur road to the top of Bench Mark Mountain, was narrowly averted in the 1960s.

15 Evergreen Mountain

Round trip: 3 miles
Hiking time: 2–3 hours
High point: 5587 feet
Elevation gain: 1300 feet
Hikable: August–October
Use: Light
Maps: Green Trails No. 143 Monte Cristo; USGS Evergreen Mountain

Driving directions: Turn north off Highway 2 for Index and drive 14.8 miles up the Index–Galena road (also known as the North Fork road) to a four-way junction, where the pavement ends. Continue straight ahead on road 65, cross the North Fork, and in a little over 2 miles reach Jack Pass on the North Fork Sky–Beckler divide. From the pass, take road 6550 to the southeast (there may or may not be signs), and in just under a mile go left on road 6554. Not for the fainthearted driver, the 9 long, precarious miles of road 6554 cross many steep, unstable slopes. Drive slowly and carefully. It seems endless, but the road finally stops and meets the trail at the 4200-foot level.

A million-dollar road climbs high to a short trail to an original-style lookout cabin. Seattle Explorer Search and Rescue has repaired and maintained the building with material supplied by the Everett Mountaineers. You'll have to pay to get in, though; the Forest Service rents the cabin nightly. Call the Skykomish Ranger Station at (360) 677-2414 for availability.

Built in the 1960s to access marginal high-elevation timber, the cost of

Evergreen Mountain Lookout

the Evergreen Mountain road far exceeded the value of the wood that was cut. Subsequent repairs consumed even more money until the road blew out massively in 1990. Displaying a remarkable willingness to keep repeating the same mistakes, in 1998 the Forest Service took money intended for watershed rehabilitation and instead used it on yet another attempt to keep this road open. Hundreds of thousands of dollars were spent, but gravity

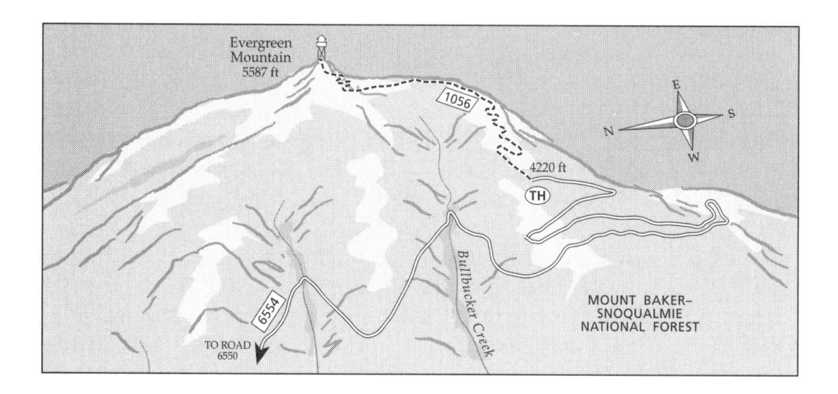

can be defied for only so long. For now it is theoretically open August 1 until October. The short season and light traffic mean that several hundred dollars of taxpayers' money have likely been spent for each airy car trip up it.

The trail starts steeply uphill through parts of a several-thousand-acre burn ignited by a logging operation in 1967. Views grow steadily, and at 5100 feet a saddle is reached and the way opens up into green, flowery meadows. In mid- to late July one can see golden arnica, glacier lilies, penstemon, lupine, columbine, and tiger lilies. A final climb reaches the summit and the 1935 vintage cabin, a room with a view. Get out the map and settle in. North is Glacier Peak with a succession of meadowy ridges in front, and to the south are the Alpine Lakes peaks and the dark forests of Johnson Ridge across the Rapid River valley. To the west is the heavily logged Beckler watershed, slowly regreening, with Eagle Rock and Spire Peak behind.

The Forest Service will not be able to keep spending the kind of money it would take to keep road 6554 open over the long term. Sooner or later reason will prevail, the road will be decommissioned, and the original trail from Rapid River to the lookout will be reopened, a longer but more rewarding and far less costly hike.

16 HEYBROOK LOOKOUT

Round trip: 2½ miles
Hiking time: 2 hours
High point: 1800 feet
Elevation gain: 1000 feet
Hikable: All year
Use: Moderate
Maps: Green Trails No. 142 Index; USGS Index

Driving directions: The trail begins right along the north side of Highway 2, just opposite a big national forest entrance sign two miles east of the Index turnoff, near milepost 37.

A short hike up from Highway 2 to an interesting old lookout atop a tower with a commanding view of Mount Index, Bridal Veil Falls, and Mount Persis. The south-facing slope that the trail climbs seldom holds much snow, making this a good winter walk.

Ascending second growth forest above the highway, the trail is a good place to see lily of the valley, vanilla leaf, bleeding heart, and, in spring, trillium. Soon the ridge, then the lookout, is reached. Dating from 1964, it is no longer used and has suffered periodic vandalism from people who smash through a gate and drive here from the Lewis Creek road.

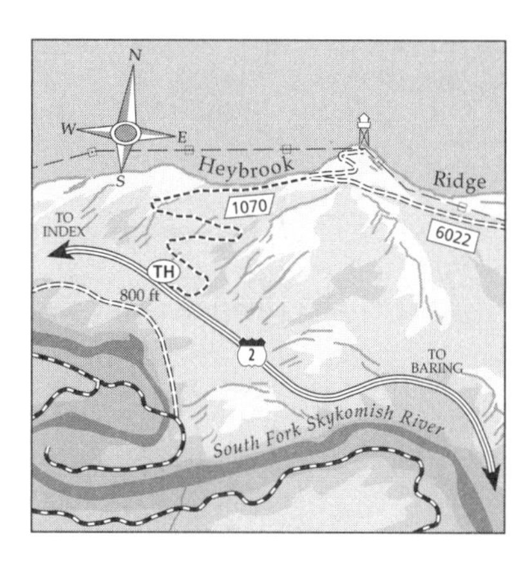

Volunteers from the Everett Mountaineers have repaired the damage, but the lookout remains at risk. The Forest Service has contemplated offering it for nightly rental; check with the Skykomish office regarding availability. It's possible to climb the stairs to just below a locked hatch leading to the walk-around deck.

The views to the south toward Mount Index are excellent, and Ragged Ridge and Gunn Peak are also visible. The forest is gradually closing off all but the southern views; the treetops, having drawn even with the top of the tower, are now overtopping it. Roads to the east provide winter ski and snowshoe opportunities.

Mount Index and Mount Persis from Heybrook Lookout

17 Barclay Lake–Eagle Lake

Round trip to Barclay Lake: 4 miles
Hiking time: 2 hours
High point: 2420 feet
Elevation gain: 220 feet
Hikable: May–November
Use: Heavy

Round trip to Eagle Lake: 8 miles
Hiking time: 6 hours
High point: 3900 feet
Elevation gain: 1700 feet
Hikable: June–October
Use: Moderate

Maps: Green Trails No. 143 Monte Cristo; USGS Baring

Driving directions: Six miles east of the Index turnoff from Highway 2, near milepost 41 at Baring, turn north across from the Baring store onto road 6024. Cross the railroad tracks and pass a few houses. Keep left at a junction at 0.3 mile and follow the logging road around the western base of Mount Baring to the trailhead at 4.4 miles, 2200 feet.

Before 1966, the popular Barclay Lake trail cut through 5 miles of some of the most spectacular ancient forest in the Skykomish region. Plans by the Forest Service and Weyerhaeuser to cut it down set off a firestorm of opposition. Although the battle was lost and barely a fragment of the forest remains, the destruction of Barclay Creek outraged the public and energized

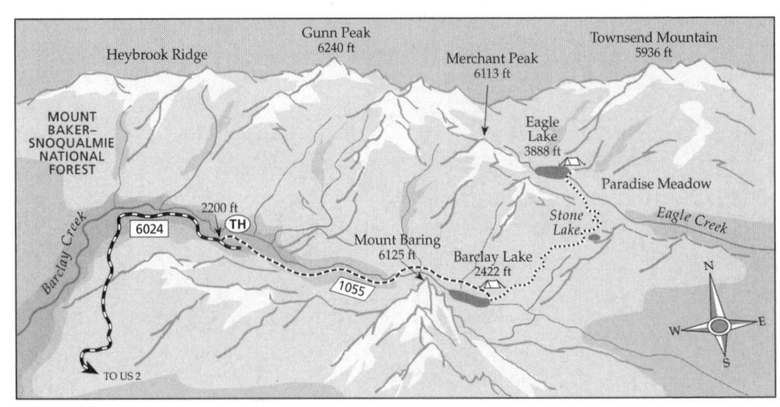

Baring Mountain from the Barclay Lake trail

a conservation movement that has gone on to protect much of the Cascades. The logging of Barclay Creek marked the high point of the timber element in the Forest Service, which has been losing ground ever since.

Barclay Lake is still well worth a visit. The remnant trail offers a short, gentle stroll, excellent for children and those who prefer their hiking on the easy side. Tucked right at the foot of the massive, nearly overhanging north wall of Mount Baring, and with Merchant Peak close to the northwest, Barclay is in one of the deeper holes in the Cascades. But there's plenty of sky to the east and west, and Barclay has none of the dark, oppressive feel of some other topographically challenged places, just a lot of very three-dimensional scenery. Weekends won't provide much solitude, but it's a great place to take visiting relatives who may not be ready for more demanding hikes but nevertheless would enjoy a real mountain experience.

The hike starts out in an old clearcut and soon enters old growth forest. Barclay Creek is crossed, and at just under 2 miles a boulder field offers views of the dark, vertical walls of Baring. This was the original "Mount Index," until that name somehow got transferred to the current holder. Baring is one of the most prominent landmarks visible from Highway 2 and can be easily identified from as far away as Everett. Both the "Baring" and "Barclay" names refer to banks, which financed the Great Northern railroad.

Boulders from the cliffs above probably dammed the creek to form Barclay Lake, which is just beyond. Underground drainage causes the lake level to drop late in the year, opening up the shores for easy walking, perfect for young hikers. Try not to let them trample the remaining lakeside vegetation. Campsites and hangout spots are plentiful. For a real show, try to be here when the summer sun is setting in the northwest—the Baring north wall is perfectly oriented for the side lighting to bring it into full relief.

For those who'd like more, Eagle Lake awaits 1500 feet above. Find the unmarked way trail at the east end of Barclay Lake, which climbs rapidly north with no thought of switchbacks. After gaining about 1400 feet in ¾ mile, pass by the very small Stone Lake. Go left through Paradise Meadow, which makes a decent attempt to live up to its name. Take care to avoid trampling the delicate wetland flowers. Marsh marigolds are abundant in June and bog gentians in early fall. In midsummer, one portion of the meadow is filled with the white spikes of blooming bog orchids. Alaska cedars, about 300 years old, abound here. About 1¾ miles beyond Barclay Lake is Eagle Lake, with a dilapidated cabin and views up to Merchant Peak and Townsend Mountain. Wandering up the gentle southwest slopes of Townsend, burned in 1930 and only slowly reforesting, brings broader views with every step.

18 LOWE CREEK ROAD

Round trip: 4–6 miles
Hiking time: 2–3 hours
High point: 900 feet
Elevation gain: 50 feet
Hikable: Usually all year
Use: Light
Maps: Green Trails No. 175 Skykomish, No. 143 Monte Cristo; USGS Grotto

Driving directions: Drive Highway 2 toward Stevens Pass, and between mileposts 45 and 46 turn right at the sign for "Money Creek Campground." Cross the river on the Old Cascade Highway, pass the

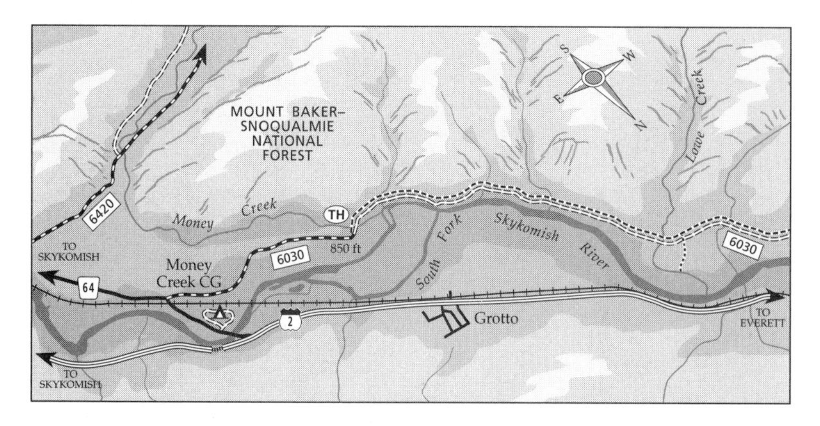

campground, and immediately after crossing the railroad tracks turn right onto the gravel Lowe Creek road. Cross several bridges. The road gets increasingly rough, and most wheels stop about a mile from the pavement. Find a place to park.

A pleasant forest stroll close to the South Fork Skykomish along an old road being reclaimed by nature. Most years it is hikable through the winter except during periods of very low snow level.

The road tunnels through second growth forest, with a viewpoint at one high spot looking across the river to old growth forests blanketing the slopes of Grotto Mountain. It then descends to closely parallel the South Fork. About a mile from where most people would park, Lowe Creek is crossed. The road crossing is long gone, but it's usually possible to boulder-hop without much trouble. Pieces of marble have been found along the creek. About ⅓ mile beyond the Lowe Creek crossing, at a blackberry- overgrown clearing, an old side road leads right a few hundred yards down to an especially nice stretch of lower Lowe Creek, where coho and chum salmon can often be seen in late fall or early winter. Farther along the "main" road, the forest grows steadily nicer, having regrown naturally following railroad logging in the 1920s, some trees now approaching 150 feet in height. About a mile and a half from Lowe Creek the road enters private property, and it's best to turn

Spawned-out coho salmon, Lowe Creek Photo by Rick McGuire

South Fork Skykomish River, Grotto Mountain behind

around before encountering the barking dogs at cabins near Index Creek.

The Forest Service is proposing to rebuild this road for the Longview Fibre Company, which would like a cheap way to haul logs off land it owns west of here. The proposal would allow Longview's trucks to barrel right through Lowe Creek, no bridge required, causing untold harm to spawning areas that the Forest Service claims do not exist. The Forest Service would spend taxpayers' money to cover most of the cost of this project, benefiting nobody but Longview Fibre. The original proposal by the current Skykomish district ranger was to do this with no environmental review at all. Quick action by conservation groups managed to keep that from happening, but the plan is still moving ahead. The conservation community will be doing all it can to protect this rare, wild area along the otherwise mostly developed South Fork Sky. Should you visit, let the Forest Service know how you feel about their plan.

19 West Fork Miller River–Coney Basin

Round trip to West Fork Miller: 9 miles
Hiking time: 5–6 hours
High point: 2400 feet
Elevation gain: 1100 feet
Hikable: May–November
Use: Light

Round trip to Coney Basin: 7 miles
Hiking time: 5 hours
High point: 3100 feet
Elevation gain: 1800 feet
Hikable: May–November
Use: Light

Maps: Green Trails No. 175 Skykomish; USGS Grotto

Driving directions: Follow Highway 2 to the turnoff signed "Money Creek Campground," between mileposts 45 and 46. Cross the river on the Old Cascade Highway, pass the campground, cross the railroad tracks, and in about a mile from Highway 2 turn right on the Miller River road 6410. In about 3.5 miles, just short of a concrete bridge over the West Fork Miller, find the old road veering off to the right. Park just off the Miller River road.

An old "mine-to-market" road, too rough for just about all vehicles, runs up the attractive West Fork Miller valley through old forest and below cliffs. The West Fork Miller option stays close to the river, or one can follow an old road/trail into scenic Coney Basin.

Pipsissewa, or prince's pine

After leaving the Miller River road, the old road soon contours above the West Fork. Attempts have been made to block it to vehicles. A few may get around the barriers, but the extremely rough road stops all but those insane enough to risk damaging their vehicles. These are

West Fork Miller River

fortunately very few in number. Follow the road for a very pleasant 2½ miles, passing several side streams and many large trees, to where an old road heads up to the right just before where the West Fork road descends to cross Coney Creek.

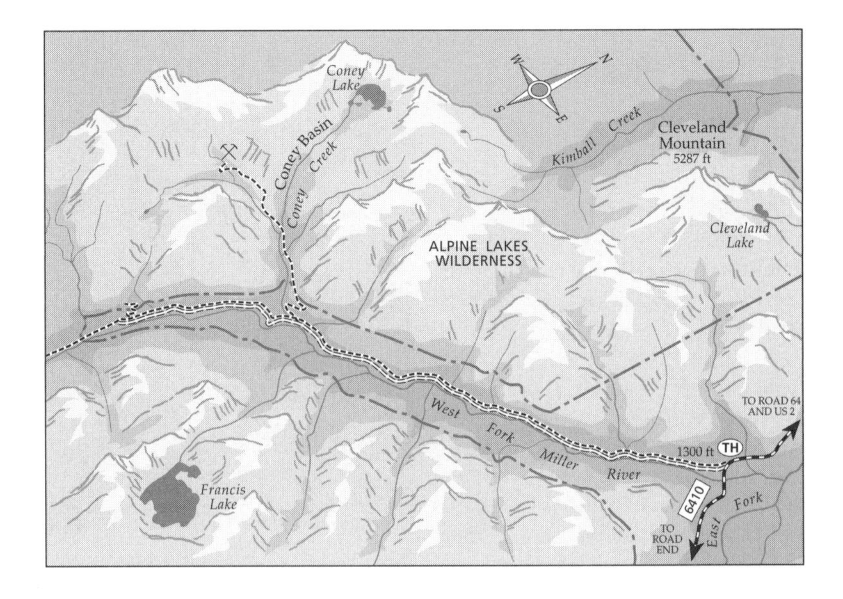

For Coney Basin, follow the old road (now mostly trail) to the right through forest along the north side of Coney Creek. The way may be faint at times, but in about ½ mile it breaks out into relatively open Coney Basin. Views and avalanche meadows abound, and one can follow a trail up to an old mine at the basin's head.

It's also possible to continue farther up the old West Fork road from the Coney junction for about another mile and a half through old growth hemlock and silver fir, and some deciduous forest. The river is accessible at several points, and there are occasional views up to the forested heights above.

20 LAKE DOROTHY

Round trip: 3 miles
Hiking time: 2–3 hours
High point: 3058 feet
Elevation gain: 800 feet
Hikable: June–October
Use: Heavy
Maps: Green Trails No. 175 Skykomish; USGS Snoqualmie Lake, Big Snow Mtn.

Driving directions: Follow Highway 2 to the turnoff signed "Money Creek Campground," between mileposts 45 and 46. Turn right onto the Old Cascade Highway, cross the river, pass the campground, cross the railroad tracks, and turn right onto the Miller River road 6410 about a mile from Highway 2. Follow the gravel road 9 miles to the trailhead, elevation 2250 feet.

The Lake Dorothy trail is a great family hike with a moderate ascent through old growth forest to a deservedly popular, island-studded lake. Those seeking more solitude can continue over a low pass to secluded Snoqualmie Lake.

From the trailhead, start upvalley through a beautiful, very old forest of Douglas fir, hemlock, and cedar, which hasn't seen a fire in nearly a thousand years. A footbridge crosses Camp Robber Creek, which plunges into a deep pool near the bridge. Smooth granitic slabs provide an attractive resting place. Beyond the bridge, the trail climbs to the outlet of Dorothy Lake, 3058 feet, 1½ miles.

The path follows above the east shore of the big lake, passing some viewpoints and campsites. It then curves around the marshy inlet area, a good place to see birds, and climbs up to a 3800-foot pass with views down to Lake Dorothy and up to Big Snow Mountain. A "shortcut" road from

Lake Dorothy

North Bend to Skykomish was planned here in the road-crazy 1960s. Common sense prevailed, but only after most of the Miller River trail was converted to road.

From the pass, the way descends to Bear Lake and Deer Lake before reaching Snoqualmie Lake, elevation 3147 feet, at 7 miles. Snoqualmie Lake can also be reached in about 7 miles from the Middle Fork Snoqualmie road via the Taylor River trail.

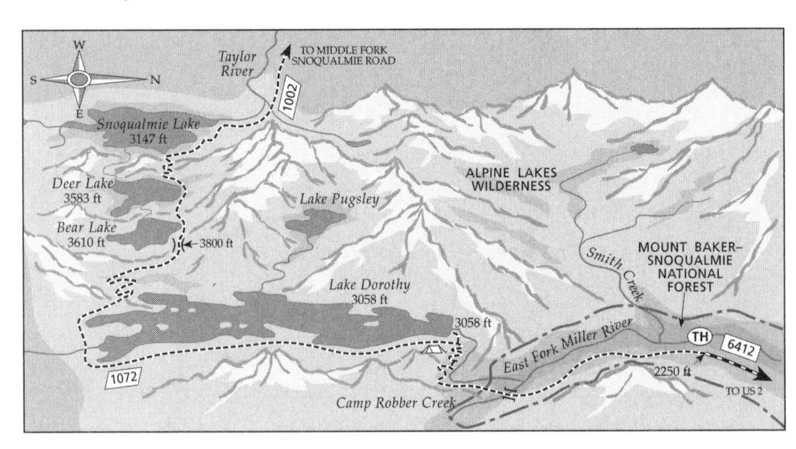

21 Johnson Ridge–Scorpion Mountain

Round trip: 10 miles
Hiking time: 6–7 hours
High point: 5540 feet
Elevation gain: 2300 feet in, 300 out
Hikable: July–October
Use: Light
Maps: Green Trails No. 143 Monte Cristo, No. 144 Bench Mark Mtn.; USGS Captain Point

Driving directions: Drive Highway 2 about ¾ mile east of the town of Skykomish and turn north on the Beckler River road 65. At 7 miles, just after the pavement ends, turn hard right on road 6520, which climbs immediately. At 2.7 miles go straight at a junction and follow the exposed, switchbacking road to its end at the trailhead in a slowly regenerating, logged moonscape 7 miles from the Beckler road.

Scorpion and Sunrise Mountains are the high points of Johnson Ridge. Don't expect a gentle, pleasant hike here. Evergreen Mountain, West Cady, and Tonga ridges all offer much easier going, but there are nice meadows and views here.

The hike starts out on an old road that climbs a hot, shadeless clearcut with one major switchback. The way is easy to lose; try to follow the most-trodden path. At about ¾ mile, the unmarked trail cuts through some brush right on the ridge top and enters the forest. The trail receives little maintenance so expect windfalls. At about 2½ miles from the start, the trail crosses the 5056-foot top of Sunrise Mountain, where the Forest Service inexplicably cut down some trees, opening up views to the north. Sunrise makes a good turnaround spot. From here the trail drops 300 feet, which seems like 3000 on the return trip, and stays close to the ridge, reaching meadows just below Scorpion

Tiger lily

Meadows on the side of Scorpion Mountain

Mountain. At a T junction, go left for the 5540-foot summit. The right fork drops to tiny Joan Lake, which can be seen below.

Flowers abound in midsummer, as do bugs. Why there seem to be so many more bugs here than in similar nearby areas is a mystery. There are also extensive huckleberry fields, which attract bears—not a good place to bring a dog. A superlative vista of the ancient forests of the upper Rapid River valley is to the east, marred only by a ridge-top clearcut on private Longview Fibre Company land to the southeast.

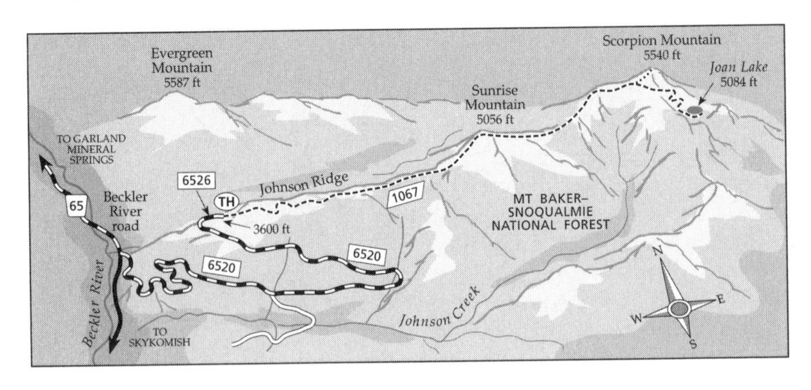

22 MEADOW CREEK–FORTUNE PONDS

Round trip: 14 miles
Hiking time: 7–8 hours
High point: 4680 feet
Elevation gain: 2700 feet
Hikable: July–October
Use: Light
Maps: Green Trails No. 144 Bench Mark Mtn.; USGS Captain Point, Bench Mark Mtn.

Driving directions: Drive Highway 2 about ¾ mile east of the town of Skykomish, turn north on the Beckler road 65, and go north 7 miles to a major junction at the pavement end. One fork goes hard right uphill; take the middle fork, road 6530, which makes a less-hard right and travels a level grade east up the Rapid River. At 4.5 miles spot the trailhead sign, and park at an elevation of 2000 feet.

Apart from some logging and 6 miles of road in the lower end, the Rapid River valley is largely wild. Extensive stretches of old growth are punctuated by burned areas. The Meadow Creek trail climbs through one of these burns into an old growth forested tributary valley, gradually climbing to ponds and views on a high shoulder of Fortune Mountain.

The Meadow Creek trail starts up an area burned in a logging-caused 1967 fire. After a mile and 1000 feet of gain, the trail turns up the valley of Meadow Creek and enters cool, 500-year-old forest comprised mostly of hemlock and silver fir. Elevation gain is gradual, the creek is crossed and recrossed, and at 4.5 miles a long swampy meadow that occupies the Meadow Creek–West Cady Creek divide is reached. The grade steepens once again before the trail swings around onto the north shoulder of Fortune Mountain. It soon arrives at picturesque lower Fortune Pond, where there are fine views over the upper West Cady country. The trail connects

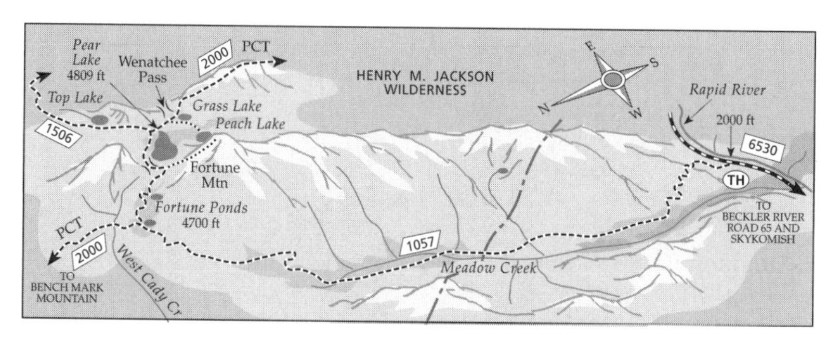

Upper Fortune Pond

with the Pacific Crest Trail, which can be followed 1 mile southeast to Pear Lake or north about 5 miles to connect with Bench Mark Mountain (Hike 11) and Pass Creek (Hike 14).

23 TONGA RIDGE

Round trip: 6 miles
Hiking time: 3–4 hours
High point: Trail, 4850 feet, Mount Sawyer, 5507 feet
Elevation gain: 500 feet
Hikable: July–October
Use: Heavy
Maps: Green Trails No. 175 Skykomish, No. 176 Stevens Pass; USGS Skykomish, Scenic

Driving directions: About 1.8 miles east of the town of Skykomish, turn south on the Foss River road 68. At 1.2 miles, keep right; at 2.4 miles, pass under a railroad bridge; and at 3.6 miles, turn left on Tonga

Ridge road 6830. After another 7 uphill miles, turn right on road 6830-310 and drive 1.1 miles to the trailhead, 4300 feet. Parking is limited; if full, backtrack ¼ mile.

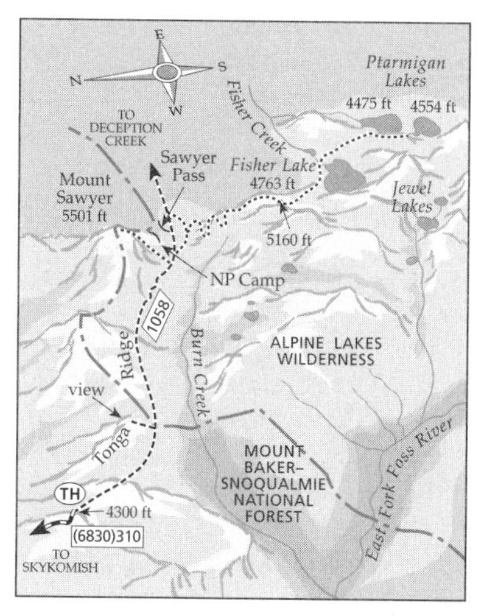

One of the most popular trips in the Skykomish region, Tonga Ridge features views, flowers, fall color, and an abundance of huckleberries. The well-maintained access road allows for a fairly short, easy hike to high country. The easy, high-elevation access makes it possible for those not up for a demanding climb to still enjoy a scenic, high ridge walk.

The Tonga Ridge trail starts out in young forest and contours along the ridge. At ¾ mile a spur trail to the left leads to a northern viewpoint. Soon after, the main trail breaks out into expansive views to the south. For the next mile, a very interesting forest

Tonga Ridge trail

and meadow ecosystem is traversed. In few other places in the Cascades can one see western red cedar, Alaska cedar, mountain hemlock, western hemlock, white pine, Douglas fir, subalpine fir, and silver fir all together in the same locale. Most of the ridge burned in 1914.

At 2 miles, a boot-beaten side path climbs a steep 750 feet, mostly through huckleberries, to the top of Mount Sawyer and all-encompassing views of the Stevens Pass area, and Glacier Peak to Mount Stuart and Mount Rainier. The main trail continues southeast to Sawyer Pass and "N.P. Camp," 3 miles from the road, in a green meadow south of the pass, which turns brilliant red in fall. Water can usually be found below here.

Another side trip is possible to Fisher and Ptarmigan Lakes. From Sawyer Pass, two separate, unofficial trails head toward Fisher Lake. At a marked junction where the official trail drops to Deception Creek, go right and then in a few feet left and follow a trail past campsites and into forest, up a hill and past two small ponds to a T junction with the other trail from Sawyer Pass. Go left, through a nice meadow, then up a short, steep gap. From here the trail descends through forest to Fisher Lake, about 2 miles from Sawyer Pass. Campsites can be found, and some faint tread leads from the outlet toward Ptarmigan Lakes.

24 East Fork Foss River–Necklace Valley

Round trip to river crossing: 10 miles
Hiking time: 4–6 hours
High point: 2160 feet
Elevation gain: 500 feet
Hikable: May–November
Use: Moderate

Round trip to Necklace Valley: 18 miles
Hiking time: 6–8 hours one way
High point: 5000 feet
Elevation gain: 3400 feet
Hikable: July–October
Use: Moderate

Maps: Green Trails No. 175 Skykomish, No. 176 Stevens Pass; USGS Skykomish, Mt. Daniel, Big Snow Mtn.

Driving directions: Turn south off Highway 2 about 1.8 miles east of the town of Skykomish and follow the Foss River road 68. At 4.2 miles, the clearly marked trailhead and parking lot are on the left.

East Fork Foss River at Burn Creek

A valley hike through appealing forest preserved in the Alpine Lakes Wilderness, the East Fork Foss is a great spring day hike or overnight backpack when snow still blankets the higher country. Deeper into the wilderness, the high Necklace Valley opens up later in the year, a demanding hike best done over 3 days or more.

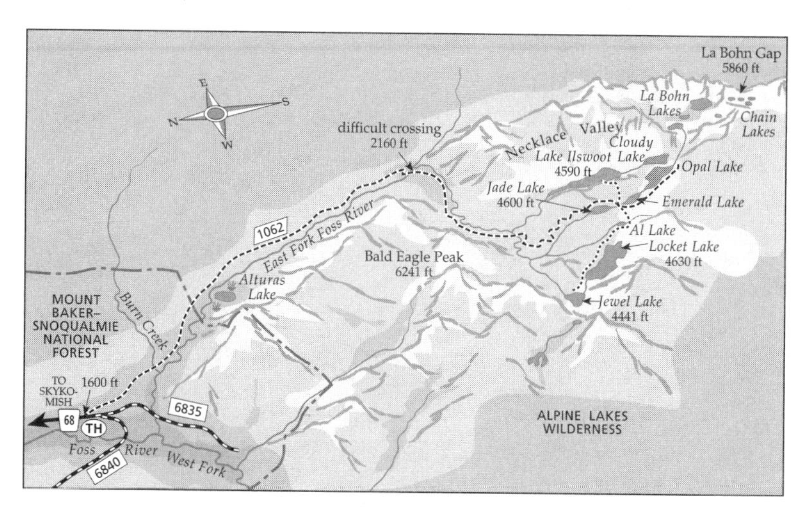

The trail starts out by traversing one of the best examples of naturally regenerated, railroad-logged, second growth forests in the Cascades. Cut in the 1930s, this beautiful forest now has many trees 2 to 3 feet in diameter and pushing 150 feet in height. Sword fern, Canadian dogwood, wild ginger, and trillium grow beneath. Forests in the Cascades usually survive one cutting fairly well, at least at low elevations, when not replanted with poorly adapted nursery-grown trees. One withdrawal from the "biomass bank" is often reparable; second or third passes are much more stressful.

Two miles in, the trail passes Alturas "Lake," really a big marsh, and trades the second growth forest for old growth forest interspersed with numerous brush fields and some open areas. At 5 miles, 2160 feet, the trail crosses the East Fork Foss (a good day hike turnaround) and starts up to Necklace Valley and its series of lakes. The first, Jade Lake, is a taxing 2½ miles and 2500 feet above. The lake names of Jade, Emerald, Opal, and Cloudy give some idea of the valley's attractiveness. But the trail beyond the river crossing is rough and muddy, and the 9 miles and 3400-foot gain in elevation to Necklace Valley are a full day's work for a strong hiker, making this a strictly multiday backpack destination. Long-distance walkers can continue across La Bohn Gap (no trail) to the upper Middle Fork Snoqualmie and CleElum countries.

25 TROUT LAKE–WEST FORK FOSS LAKES

Round trip to Trout Lake: 3 miles
Hiking time: 2 hours
High point: 2000 feet
Elevation gain: 360 feet
Hikable: May–October
Use: Heavy

Round trip to Copper Lake: 8 miles
Hiking time: 4–5 hours
High point: 3960 feet
Elevation gain: 2300 feet
Hikable: July–October
Use: Heavy

Maps: Green Trails No. 175 Skykomish, No. 176 Stevens Pass; USGS Skykomish, Big Snow Mtn.

Driving directions: About 1.8 miles east of the town of Skykomish, turn south from Highway 2 onto the Foss River road 68 and follow it past the turnoff for Tonga Ridge and the East Foss trail to road 6835, about 4.5 miles from the highway. Turn left and drive 2 miles to the trailhead.

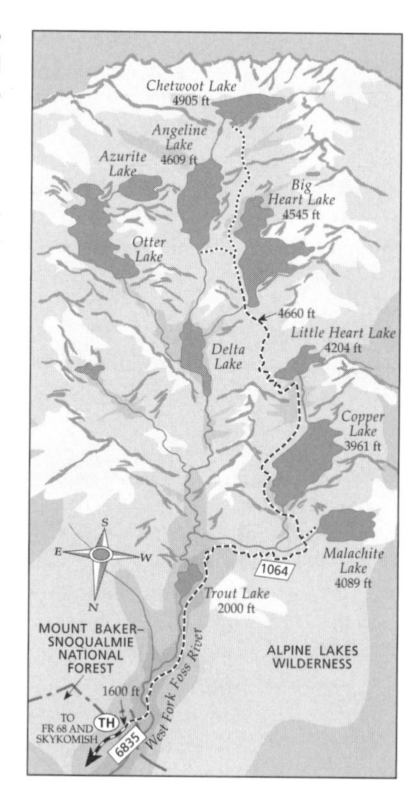

The West Fork Foss trail leads into the heart of the Alpine Lakes, the area that gave a name to the greater Alpine Lakes Wilderness. Trout Lake offers an easy walk, Copper Lake is a longer day hike, and numerous others lie beyond in the realm of backpacking. It's easy to see why the place is popular; don't look for solitude here.

The hike starts on an old railroad grade, which soon enters the Alpine Lakes Wilderness and becomes a trail. The river, where salmon can occasionally be seen, is crossed on two footbridges and a short section of huge trees is passed, including one particularly enormous Douglas fir. Soon Trout Lake is reached, elevation 2000 feet,

Tributary on the trail to Copper Lake

1½ miles from the road. A 1991 landslide raised the lake level, killing some trees—an interesting example of how these mountains are still a work in progress.

From Trout Lake, the way steepens through trees and open areas. Water and waterfalls are plentiful. At 3½ miles a trail heads right for ¼ mile to the rocky cirque of Malachite Lake. The left fork crosses several streams and shortly arrives at Copper Lake. The large, beautiful lake has numerous designated campsites, and the best lunch spots are scattered near the outlet.

For those wanting more, it's possible to continue past Little Heart Lake, follow the trail above it, and take a side trail that branches left just as the main trail starts to descend. The side trail leads to a spectacular view from a rocky promontory looking north down the Foss valley to the Skykomish. Glacier Peak is in the distance, and Delta and Otter Lakes sit below. Many other explorations are possible for those with overnight gear.

26 BECKLER PEAK

Round trip: 5 miles
No trail
Hiking time: 4–6 hours
High point: 5062 feet
Elevation gain: 2000 feet
Hikable: July–October
Use: Light
Maps: USGS Skykomish, Scenic

Driving directions: Drive Highway 2 to a little over 3 miles east of the town of Skykomish and turn north on road 6066, just past milepost 52. The turnoff is not easy to spot and is located at a hazardous place for left turns, just after where a hill with double eastbound lanes tops out. If you miss it or if traffic is close behind, keep going east to a safe turnaround spot and approach it westbound. Once on the gravel road, pass under powerlines and follow it west for about 2 level miles to where it starts switchbacking up the southwest slopes of Beckler. The generally well-kept road tops out just under 3000 feet and makes a long, nearly level traverse to the east across the south slopes of Beckler, reaching a junction with road 6067 about 7 miles from the highway. Go left and park on road 6066, where a washout stops traffic in less than 0.5 mile.

Back in 1924 a trail, now mostly gone, was built to a fire lookout, now vanished, on the west summit of Beckler Peak. Conservation and recreation groups have proposed building a new trail to the east summit of Beckler and its 360-degree views. The Forest Service had funding for this in the

Harlan Creek clearcut north of Beckler Peak; Mount Fernow behind, snowy Chiwaukum Mountains in the distance Photo by John Roper

mid-1990s but was unwilling to take the steps necessary (preserving nearby habitat) for it to conform to new grizzly bear habitat protection rules and abandoned the project, losing the funding. Hopefully a more imaginative approach will someday be tried and this trail will get built. Although bits of the old trail can be found, it is for now a trip only for those experienced

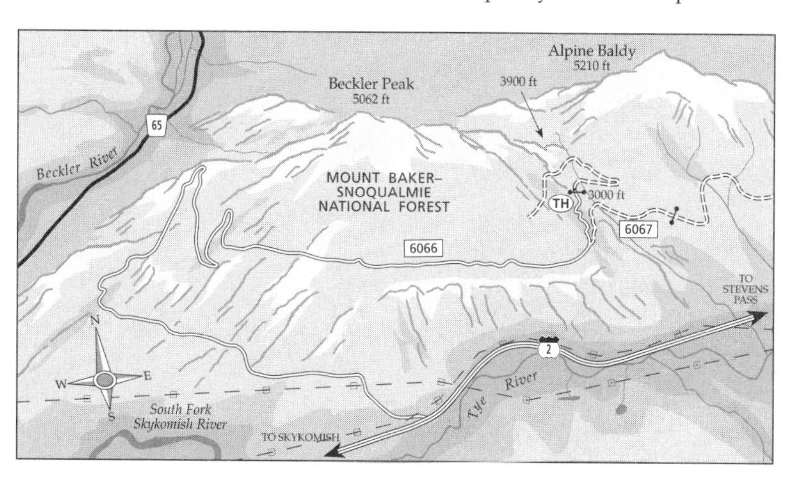

Cow parsnip

in navigating through trailless old growth forests (and brush).

The old lookout was on a tower on the west summit, which now has no views. The east summit has excellent views, but the old trail doesn't go to it. Only a short, overgrown segment of the trail is on the route from the road to the east summit, making Beckler a cross-country hike. The basic idea is to go to the 3900-foot low point on the ridge between Beckler and Alpine Baldy, then head up and west. There's no avoiding the extensive brush along the abandoned road and in logged areas. Although the old lookout site is also brushy, the elegant trail work through a field of huge boulders just east of it is worth seeing. A cliff band makes it very difficult to traverse directly between the east summit and the lookout site; the trail crosses considerably below.

A new trail to the east summit would be a real attraction, Beckler Peak having some of the best views in this part of the Cascades. The panoply of the Alpine Lakes peaks to the south is tremendous. The only jarring note is the 2-square-mile moonscape of the Harlan Creek clearcut to the north, cut by Weyerhaeuser and later traded to the national forest. One of the largest and most brutal logging jobs of recent decades in this area, the high-elevation forest will take centuries to regenerate.

27 Iron Goat Trail

One way: 6¾ miles
Hiking time: 3–5 hours
High point: 3100 feet
Elevation gain (or loss): 800 feet
Hikable: May–November
Use: Moderate
Maps: On reader boards at trailheads; brochure available from the Forest Service and elsewhere; online maps at *www.irongoat.org;* Green Trails No. 176 Stevens Pass

Driving directions: For the west trailhead, at Martin Creek, take Highway 2 to milepost 55, 6 miles east of the town of Skykomish. Turn left (north) on the Old Cascade Highway, road 67, and follow it as it heads east 2.3 miles to the Martin Creek road 6710. Turn left again and drive 1.4 miles to the well-marked trailhead. The east trailhead, at Wellington, can be reached by turning north off Highway 2 onto the Old Cascade Highway at milepost 64.3, just west of the Stevens Pass summit. If coming from the west, it is usually safer to go to the top of the pass, turn around, and approach the turnoff from the east. Follow the old highway 2.8 miles to the junction with Forest Service road 050 and turn right for the parking lot.

Parts of the original route of the Great Northern railroad, which first crossed Stevens Pass in 1893, have been converted into a nearly level, scenic and historic trail. This is the only such place that has been preserved for hikers: the Milwaukee Road grade at Snoqualmie Pass is really a gated service road, and the Naches Wagon Trail is clobbered by ORVs and jeeps. Compared to these, the Iron Goat is a delight.

The trail can be hiked from either end or through one way if a car shuttle can be arranged. Portions of it are barrier-free. The Iron Goat trail is the product of many hours of volunteer labor. For complete information and historical background, buy a copy of the *The Iron Goat Trail: A Guidebook,*

Railroad tunnel on the Iron Goat Trail

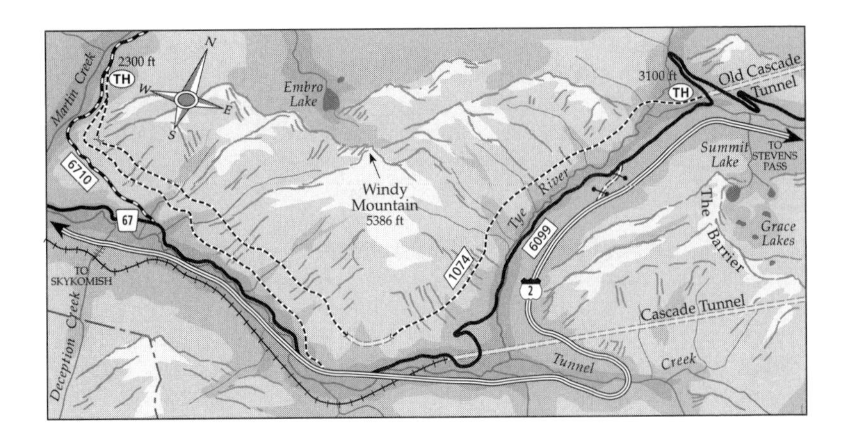

from The Mountaineers Books. Or check out the website: *www.irongoat.org*. (This is the only trail in this guidebook with its own website.)

Maps and informational signs can be found at both trailheads. From Martin Creek, it is possible to follow the railroad grade/trail past a couple of short tunnels (the tunnels are blocked, and it's highly recommended to stay out of them) to the shoofly path around the ½-mile Windy Point tunnel and a cleared viewpoint 3¼ miles from the start. A good option for the return trip is to descend the signed "Corea Cutoff" trail and follow it back to the trailhead. From the Wellington trailhead, it's a scenic 3 miles or so of barrier-free trail to reach the Windy Point tunnel, and side trips can also be made to the first Stevens Pass tunnel and the site of the 1910 Wellington disaster, where nearly a hundred people died in an avalanche. Maybe some of their ghosts still linger.

28 KELLY CREEK

Round trip: 9 miles
Hiking time: 5–6 hours
High point: 5000 feet
Elevation gain: 2000 feet
Hikable: July–October
Use: Light
Maps: Green Trails No. 144 Bench Mark Mtn., No. 176 Stevens Pass; USGS Scenic, Captain Point

Driving directions: Take Highway 2 to milepost 55, 6 miles east of the town of Skykomish. Turn left (north) on the Old Cascade Highway, road 67, and follow it as it heads east 2.3 miles to the Martin Creek road

6710. Turn left again and drive 1.4 miles to the well-marked Martin Creek trailhead. This trailhead may one day be the access for Kelly Creek, but for now it is possible to drive another 1.9 miles on the Martin Creek road to a junction with road (6710)230. Cross Martin Creek and find a place to park.

A long-abandoned trail climbing an old growth forested valley to scenic meadows below Captain Point. Most of the trail is easy to follow, and volunteers occasionally do some work on it. It may be officially reopened one day.

View from the Kelly Creek trail

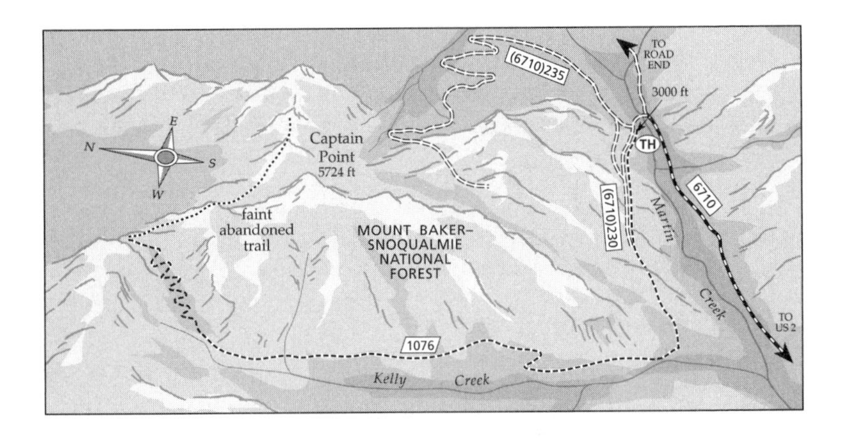

From the parking area, a very overgrown logging track goes west and skirts the base of a clearcut for almost 1 mile. At the edge of the clearcut the track becomes trail, enters forest, and turns north to parallel Kelly Creek. The trail ascends the Kelly Creek valley through old forest of hemlock and silver fir. Old puncheon and blazes testify to its age. Near the 3½-mile point, the trail starts switchbacking up the valley headwall. It soon crests the ridge and at an old sign meets the abandoned "North Crest" trail. Heather and huckleberry meadows on the north side of Captain Point can be seen. The old trail can be followed right as it contours the meadows to a saddle east of Captain Point, where a short bushwhack north leads to an unnamed peak with extensive views. Another option is to follow faint tread up the north ridge of Captain Point from the sign near where the Kelly Creek trail meets the North Crest trail on the ridge top.

29 DECEPTION CREEK

Round trip: 10 miles to Fisher Creek
Hiking time: 5–6 hours
High point: 3150 feet
Elevation gain: 1150 feet
Hikable: May–November
Use: Light
Maps: Green Trails No. 176 Stevens Pass; USGS Scenic

Driving directions: The turnoff to the Deception Creek road 6088 is about 0.2 mile east of the Deception Falls parking lot, about 8.2 miles east of the town of Skykomish. There may be no sign. Follow the road about a quarter mile to the trailhead parking area.

Deception Creek, in the Alpine Lakes Wilderness

A big, forested valley, the most extensive stretch of ancient forest in the Alpine Lakes Wilderness. The trail is low enough to allow early season hiking when higher country is still buried in snow. The views are beyond day-hiking range, so go for the deep forest experience.

The trail immediately enters old growth and stays near cascading Deception Creek. At ½ mile the creek is crossed on a new bridge and the trail

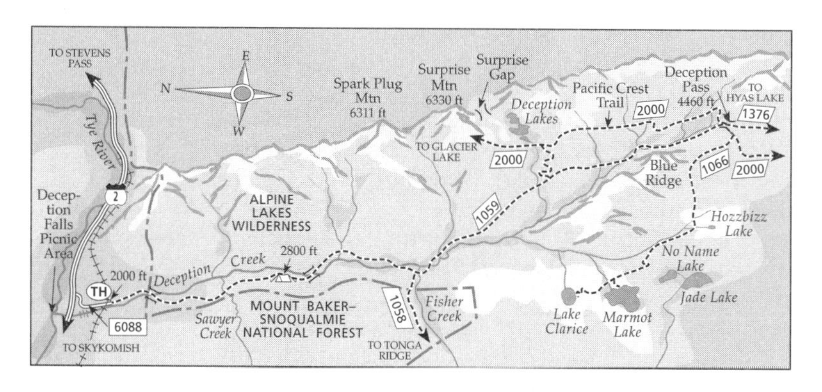

starts to climb. Most of the modest elevation gain comes in the next 2 miles as the trail passes through nice old growth forest.

Sawyer Creek is crossed at 2½ miles, and a creekside camp spot is encountered at 3 miles. Deception Creek is crossed on a rustic bridge and then recrossed. At 5 miles is a junction with the Tonga Ridge trail dropping from the west. Just beyond the junction the trail crosses Fisher Creek, a logical turnaround spot for the day hiker. But much remains, and the forest actually gets more impressive for a few more miles, having grown up following a fire that burned in 1668. The valley broadens toward its head and starts to feel drier as it approaches Deception Pass and the upper Cle Elum watershed. There were once plans to log the forests and push a road across the pass, but the efforts of motivated defenders made sure that never happened.

30 Surprise Creek

Round trip: 10 miles to Glacier Lake
Hiking time: 6 hours
High point: 4806 feet
Elevation gain: 2600 feet
Hikable: July–October
Use: Heavy
Maps: Green Trails No. 176 Stevens Pass; USGS Scenic

Driving directions: Turn south off Highway 2 at Scenic, milepost 58.7, just under 10 miles east of the town of Skykomish, and just before the highway passes over the railroad tracks at the west portal of the Stevens Pass tunnel. The road descends and passes over the railroad tracks. Turn right and follow it for 0.2 mile to the trailhead sign, elevation 2200 feet.

Surprise Creek offers a pleasant if relentlessly uphill walk through old growth forest to two large, rock-rimmed lakes. A good day hike, this is also the entrance for several loop or one-way backpack trips.

The trail starts out up a powerline access road for 1⁄10 mile to the junction with the real foot trail. For the next mile the trail passes through tremendous old growth forest, vintage 1508, cool and moist even on the hottest day. In 1976 the Alpine Lakes Wilderness protected this forest, which, incredibly, had been scheduled for cutting. At 1½ miles, Surprise Creek is crossed, and the trail route begins to alternate between forest and avalanche brush, uphill all the way. The trail climbs the valley's headwall, and at just over 4 miles passes a junction with the Trap Pass trail and reaches deep blue, mountain-rimmed Surprise Lake.

Numerous designated campsites can be found, but don't expect solitude.

Surprise Lake

Less crowded Glacier Lake can be visited about a mile farther up. Above Glacier Lake the trail breaks out of the forest into a rocky basin and climbs to Surprise Gap and splendid views south to Mounts Hinman and Daniel. One can descend from here to interestingly shaped Deception Lakes, making a loop return to near Glacier Lake on the Crest Trail, or head on farther south to broad Deception Pass.

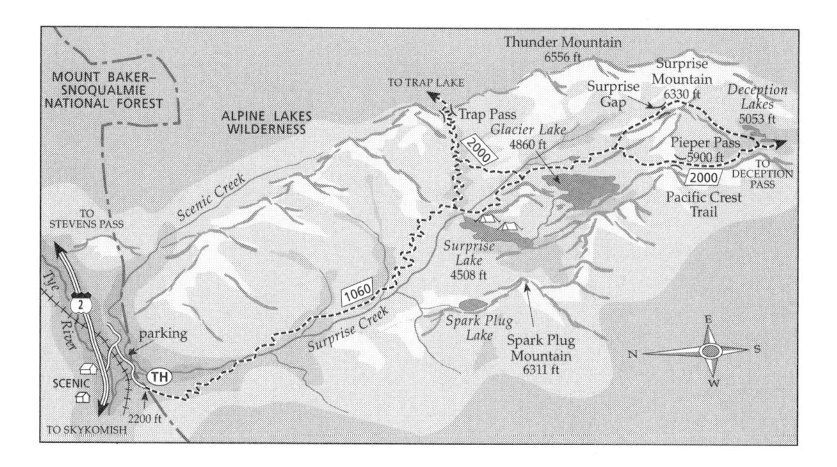

31 Hope Lake and Mig Lake

Round trip to Mig Lake: 4 miles
Hiking time: 2–3 hours
High point: 4660 feet
Elevation gain: 1660 feet
Hikable: July–October
Use: Moderate
Maps: Green Trails No. 176 Stevens Pass; USGS Stevens Pass

Driving directions: From Skykomish, drive Highway 2 east about 12 miles. The highway makes a big, sweeping, 180-degree turn as it crosses Tunnel Creek. Just after the creek, turn right onto road 6095, possible only from the eastbound lanes; if coming from the east, go past the exit, turn around safely, and approach it eastbound. At 0.6 mile the road forks. Go right on road 6095, crossing a cement bridge over Tunnel Creek. At 0.8 mile, the next junction, go straight ahead, avoiding a second bridge. At 1.2 miles, the road splits again. Go steeply left on road (6095)115 and at 1.3 miles find the Tunnel Creek trailhead, elevation 3200 feet.

The short Tunnel Creek trail intersects the Crest Trail at Hope Lake, which can be followed north to heather- and huckleberry-surrounded Mig Lake, one of the more interesting names in the Cascades. Is it for the Mikoyan–Gurevitch state aeronautic design bureau, creators of Russia's famous MiG fighter jets? No MiGs have ever flown here; most of the low-flying jets that explosively appear in this part of the Cascades are aptly named Grumman A-6 "Intruders" and are from Whidbey Naval Air Station.

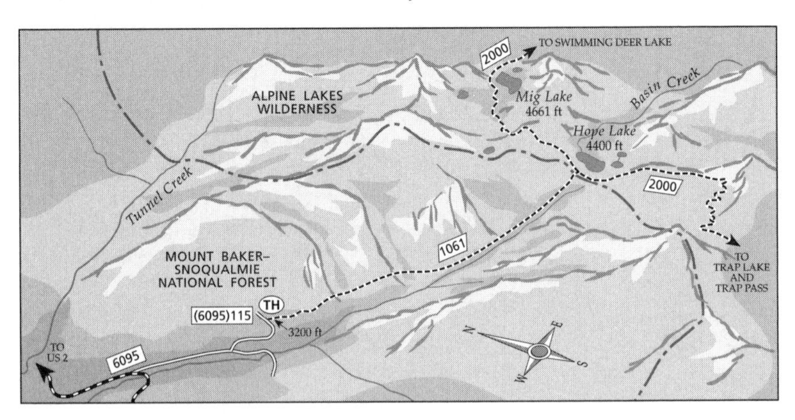

Cotton grass at Mig Lake

The trail starts in a clearcut but soon enters old growth forest, gaining elevation steadily, passing some rock slides. At 1½ miles it reaches the Cascade Crest and the Pacific Crest Trail at Hope Lake, elevation 4400 feet. From Hope Lake, the Crest Trail can be followed right (west) across a scenic south-facing slope. At 5¼ miles from the Tunnel Creek parking area, it reaches an unmarked junction, where an unofficial trail drops left into the Trap Lake cirque. The Crest Trail continues straight ahead to Trap Pass and more views before descending to Surprise Creek (Hike 30).

From Hope Lake, the left option climbs 200 feet to Mig Lake. Set in an appealing meadow surrounded by subalpine forest, Mig Lake is interesting for more than its name. Many types of flowers grow here, some of them very unusual, including cottongrass. The trail can be followed beyond Mig as it contours through a basin and then above Swimming Deer Lake to a series of small lakes and pocket meadows above Josephine Lake, which can also be reached by hiking south from Stevens Pass (Hike 33).

32 Grace Lakes

Round trip: 5 miles
Hiking time: 2–3 hours
High point: 4800 feet
Elevation gain: 800 feet
Hikable: July–October
Use: Moderate
Maps: Green Trails No. 176 Stevens Pass (no trail shown); USGS Stevens Pass (no trail shown)

Driving directions: Drive to Stevens Pass, the high point of Highway 2, and just west of the summit, turn into the first ski area parking lot. Go to the west end of the upper parking lot. The lot is often gated, and even if it isn't, it could be before you return, so it's best to park below the gate.

Pleasant heather-surrounded small lakes can be found on both sides of Stevens Pass. On the south, Grace Lakes comprise four small tarns, with larger Summit Lake nearby. Although the ski area makes an unattractive approach, it can't be seen from the lakes, and the start from Stevens Pass means that high country is reached with a minimum of physical effort.

From the gate below the parking area, walk uphill into the ski area.

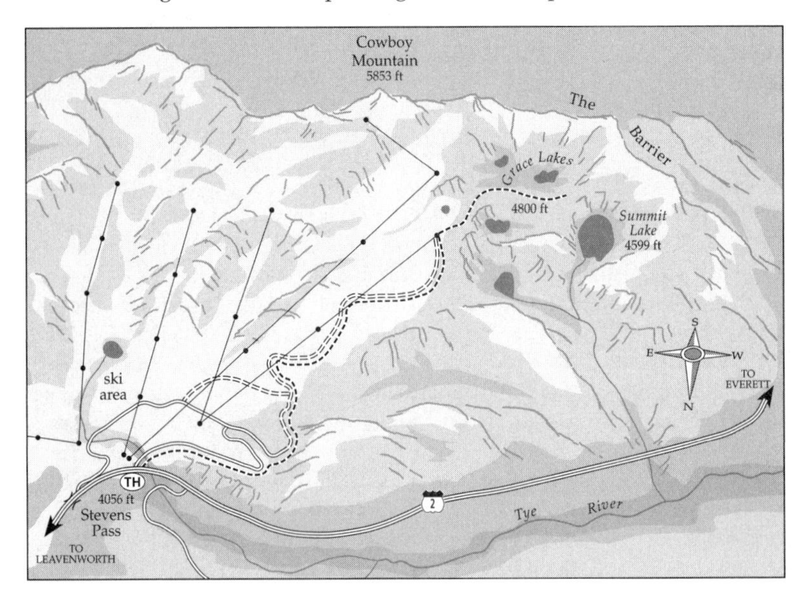

One of the Grace Lakes

Follow the service road beneath and beside the "Green" chairlift as it grinds up to the very top of the lift, elevation 4800 feet. But the views grow steadily, and soon the grind is over. The lakes trail is directly behind the top of the lift.

A heather-lined path drops downhill to the first lake, with other paths taking off from there to the other lakes. Summit Lake can be found down one of the paths, across a rock slide. Silver fir and mountain hemlock forest surrounds the lakes, and the ski area seems far away.

33 LAKE SUSAN JANE AND JOSEPHINE LAKE

Round trip: 8 miles
Hiking time: 6–7 hours
High point: 5080 feet
Elevation gain: 1370 in, 400 out
Hikable: July–October
Use: Moderate to heavy
Maps: Green Trails No. 176 Stevens Pass; USGS Stevens Pass

Driving directions: Drive to Stevens Pass, the high point of Highway 2, where signs indicate where to park and where not to.

The stretch of the Pacific Crest Trail south from Stevens Pass climbs through a ski area and drops under powerlines to a service road before getting to the good stuff. Still, it's a worthwhile hike through high forests, huckleberry fields, and lakes and pocket meadows.

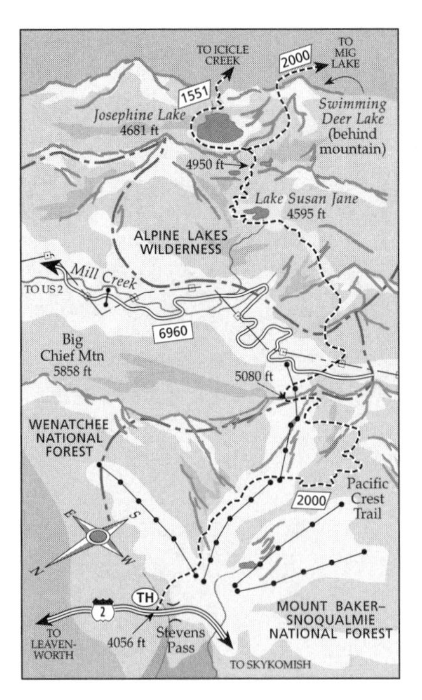

The Crest Trail starts up the slope south of the main buildings, lavishly built, and climbs above the ski area to a 5080-foot pass into the Mill Creek drainage. It then drops a quarter of a mile to cross under powerlines from Chief Joseph Dam on the Columbia before heading back into forest and traversing some rock slides with views down Mill Creek to Nason Ridge. At 3½ miles is the rocky cirque of Lake Susan Jane. The trail climbs beyond the lake to an interesting high bench perched above Josephine Lake. Several small lakes and meadows can be explored here, and one can wander up nearby hilltops. The Stuart range can be seen to the southeast. It's also possible to follow the Crest Trail southwest toward Mig Lake (Hike 31) or take the trail descending clockwise into

Pacific Crest Trail near Lake Susan Jane

the round bowl where sits Josephine Lake. Longer-distance options lead to Whitepine Creek and the Icicle valley from here.

34 Skyline Lake

Round trip: 3 miles
Hiking time: 2 hours
High point: 5092 feet
Elevation gain: 1050 feet
Hikable: July–October
Use: Moderate
Maps: Green Trails No. 176 Stevens Pass, No. 144 Bench Mark Mtn. (trail not shown); USGS Stevens Pass, Labyrinth Mtn.

Driving directions: Drive to Stevens Pass, the high point of Highway 2. The parking situation at Stevens Pass changes periodically, but signs should indicate where it is not frowned upon.

This huckleberry-surrounded lake sits on a high shelf just north of Stevens Pass. In summer, a steep jeep track gives access. The area is a popular

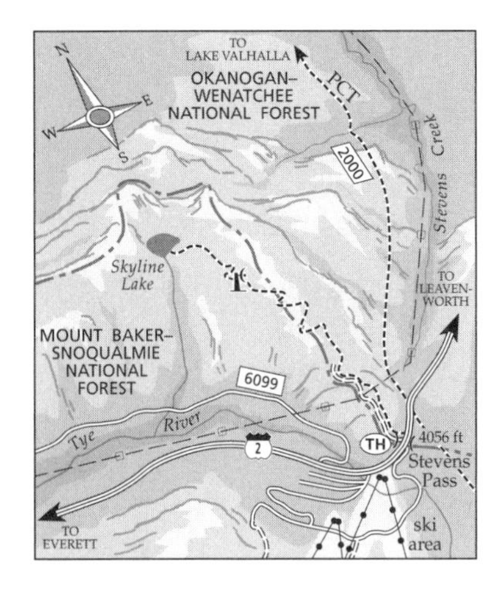

winter snowshoe and ski destination with the plowed highway below making it a short trip to high country.

Just behind the buildings north of the highway, find an unsigned road going uphill to a steep jeep track, which climbs the rib from the pass north. A radio tower is soon passed, and another short climb brings one to the lake. The berries ripen in mid-August. For broader views, climb the ridge to the west of the lake. Take care to come back the way you went up. Note that steep loose slopes directly below and south of the lake could be dangerous.

Skyline Lake

35 LAKE VALHALLA: PACIFIC CREST TRAIL

Round trip: 11 miles
Hiking time: 6 hours
High point: 5100 feet
Elevation gain: 1400 feet in, 500 feet out
Hikable: July–October
Use: Lake Valhalla heavy, PCT moderate
Maps: Green Trails No. 144 Bench Mark Mtn.; USGS Labyrinth Mtn.

Driving directions: Drive to Stevens Pass, the high point of Highway 2. The parking at Stevens Pass changes from time to time, but signs usually show where it is permissible.

North from Stevens Pass, the Pacific Crest Trail follows the original route of the Great Northern Railway from the top of Stevens Pass down into the Nason Creek valley. Although of historical interest, the route down the railroad grade skirts along closely opposite the noisy highway, losing about 300 feet of elevation in just under 2 very long shadeless miles. The trail beyond into the Nason Creek headwaters is a pleasant walk, but the trail section near the highway is even less enjoyable on the uphill return.

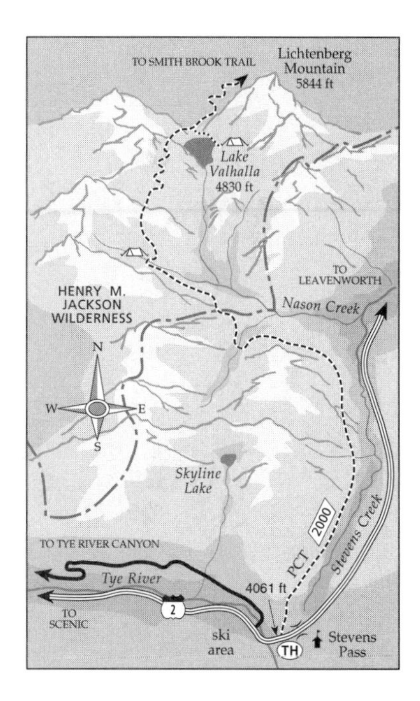

Find the Pacific Crest Trail between an electric substation and a green A-frame building north of the highway. The Great Northern abandoned this route after completion of the first Stevens Pass tunnel in 1900. After what seems like an eternity near the highway, the trail swings into the forested Nason Creek valley and leaves the noise behind. At 3 miles it crosses into the Henry M. Jackson Wilderness and at 3½ enters a basin of wet meadows with a good campsite.

From here the way ascends an easy 5050-foot spur, and a side trail drops into the Lake Valhalla Basin. Heavily used camps can be found, the best being near the outlet end. Most hikers, sensibly, come here via Smith Brook trail (Hike 36). The Crest Trail can be followed to a pass northeast of the lake, and heather meadows can be climbed to the east up 5844-foot Lichtenberg Mountain.

Lake Valhalla

36 SMITH BROOK–LAKE JANUS

Round trip: 7 miles
Hiking time: 5–7 hours
High point: 4700 feet
Elevation gain: 650 feet in, 750 feet out, to Lake Janus
Hikable: July–October
Use: Heavy
Maps: Green Trails No. 144 Bench Mark Mtn.; USGS Labyrinth Mtn.

Driving directions: Drive Highway 2 east from Stevens Pass 4.1 miles and turn north on the Smith Brook road 6700. Follow it 3.2 miles north to the trailhead, at 4200 feet.

Smith Brook offers a short link to the Pacific Crest Trail, which can be followed south to crowded Lake Valhalla (must be the name) or north to slightly less-crowded Lake Janus.

Smith Brook trail starts up a brushy hillside before entering forest and intersecting the Pacific Crest Trail at Union Gap, 1 mile, 4700 feet. To the left, the PCT can be followed along a level contour for about a mile, then it climbs 400 feet in ¾ mile before descending to Lake

Lake Janus

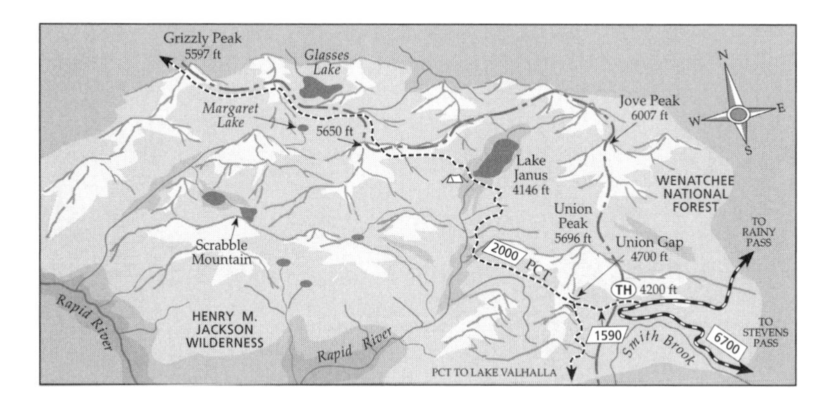

Valhalla at 4830 feet. Good views of the Stevens Pass area can be had, and the lake is less crowded on weekdays.

From Union Gap, the PCT north drops 650 feet into the upper Rapid River Basin before climbing a short stretch to scenic Lake Janus. Janus is surrounded by meadows and tall trees, with 6007-foot Jove Peak close above. The easy access means it, too, can get crowded on weekends. For more views, follow the Crest Trail 1½ miles west to a ridge from where it's possible to hike or scramble up to a 5650-foot summit with vistas all around.

Glacier lily

37 Minotaur Lake

Round trip: 4 miles
Hiking time: 2–3 hours
High point: 5550 feet
Elevation gain: 1750 feet
Hikable: July–October
Use: Moderate
Maps: Green Trails No. 144 Bench Mark Mtn.; USGS Labyrinth Mtn.

Driving directions: About 4.1 miles east of Stevens Pass, turn north on the Smith Brook road 6700. Follow it past the Union Gap trailhead and over Rainy Pass. At 5 miles the road reaches a junction; turn left to continue on road 6700. Descend to cross Rainy Creek, and at 6.9 miles from the highway turn left onto road 6704. Go 6.9 miles to the easily missed trailhead at elevation 3800 feet.

A trail so steep that it might better be called a route, to a lake with pretty islands, surrounded by white granitic cliffs. Nearby Theseus Lake is named

Minotaur Lake, Henry M. Jackson Wilderness

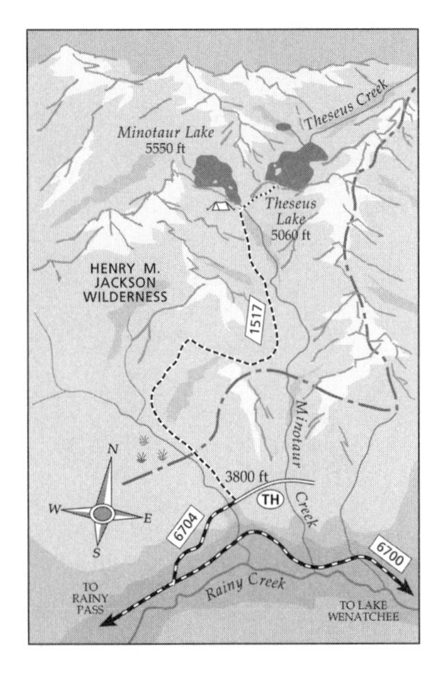

for the mythical hero who slew the Minotaur, a fearsome monster kept by the king of Crete in the terrifying Labyrinth, after which the mountain here is named.

The newly rebuilt trail starts out climbing and keeps going up for 1 mile before leveling out and traversing forest to the east. It then swings into the valley of Minotaur Creek and climbs through huckleberry meadows and mountain hemlock forest to Minotaur Lake, at 5550 feet. The best viewpoint is on the ridge to the right of and just above the lake and shouldn't be missed. Below to the northeast lies 5060-foot Theseus Lake and its island. The views to Labyrinth Mountain and across the Little Wenatchee are also excellent. A steep trail drops down to Theseus Lake, but the ridge viewpoint makes a better lunch spot.

38 LANHAM LAKE

Round trip: 3 miles
Hiking time: 4 hours
High point: 4143 feet
Elevation gain: 1100 feet
Hikable: Late June–October
Use: Light
Maps: Green Trails No. 176 Stevens Pass; USGS Labyrinth Mtn.

Driving directions: Heading eastbound, 6 miles east of Stevens Pass look for signs for the Stevens Pass Nordic Ski Area at Mill Creek. If driving westbound, look for signs and a turnoff leading south near milepost 70. Park in the flat area just off the highway, walk up the road a couple hundred feet, and find the trailhead to the left.

Lanham Lake provides a short, steep hike to a small lake tucked deep in a north-facing valley below Jim Hill Mountain, named for the robber-baron builder of the Great Northern Railway.

Lanham Lake and Jim Hill Mountain

The trail starts out in nice woods but climbs under a powerline and crosses a service road. The way then follows an old logging spur before entering old growth forest again. It stays within sight and sound of Lanham Creek, through silver fir and hemlock forest, the rest of the way to Lanham Lake. At 4143 feet, it's a shallow lake in a deep valley, and about the only further exploration possible is to circle the lake, crossing a marshy area at the inlet.

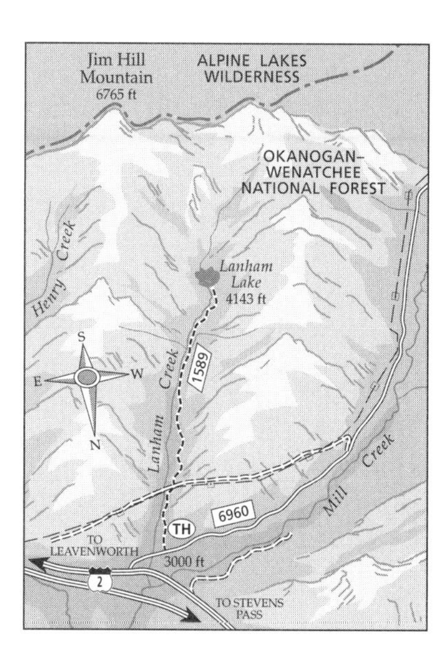

Jim Hill Mountain towers to the southeast. Although fully deserving of the "robber baron" epithet, Hill also had a human side. He ordered that hoboes be tolerated on Great Northern freight trains as long as they did no harm, recognizing their role in helping to build the railroad. This tolerance lasted for decades, surviving even the merger with Northern Pacific, which led to the creation of the Burlington Northern Railway in the 1970s. Sadly, the

1990s merger, which formed the Burlington Northern–Santa Fe, erased Jim Hill from "his" railroad. His last surviving echo is the name of the "Empire Builder" Amtrak train from Seattle to Chicago. The train can be seen heading east along the Stevens Pass line in the early evening.

39 Snowy Creek–Rock Mountain

Round trip: 9 miles
Hiking time: 6 hours
High point: 6852 feet
Elevation gain: 3250 feet
Hikable: July–October
Use: Moderate
Maps: Green Trails No. 144 Bench Mark Mtn., No. 145 Wenatchee Lake; USGS Mount Howard

Driving directions: Turn north off Highway 2 at 4.1 miles east of Stevens Pass. Follow the Smith Brook road 6700 past the Union Gap trailhead and over Rainy Pass to a junction at 3.5 miles. Continue straight on road 6705 for another 3.5 miles to the trailhead at 3600 feet.

Flower-filled meadows, an ice-blue lake, and spectacular summit views are all to be found on Rock Mountain. Two approaches are possible: a south-side route going straight up from Highway 2 and mostly in the sun (see Hike 40), and this one, starting 900 feet higher from Snowy Creek, ascending much of the way through shady forests.

The Snowy Creek route starts out in old growth with mountain views opening up in about a mile. At about 2 miles, 4600 feet, a pleasant basin

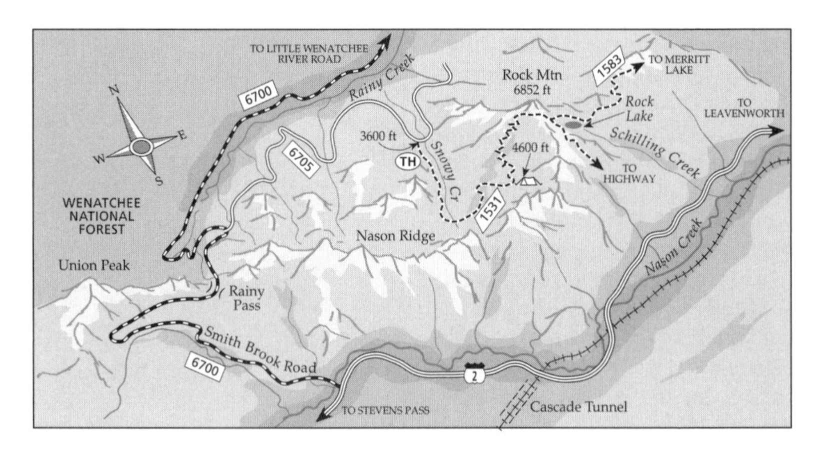

meadow offers good camping. From here, the way switchbacks up through cool open forest, gradually emerging into an infinity of flowers on the upper slopes. On the 6600-foot ridge, the trail reaches a junction with the south-side route and makes the final climb to the 6852-foot summit.

The summit views are truly grand. To the north, Sloan Peak and Glacier Peak stand out, to the southwest the top of Mount Rainier can be seen above Mount Daniel, and Mount Stuart dominates the southeast beyond the Chiwaukums. Pesky mountain goats, inexplicably transplanted here from the Olympics, can sometimes be a bother.

View from the top of Rock Mountain

40 Rock Mountain–Rock Lake

Round trip: 11 miles
Hiking time: 8 hours
High point: 6852 feet
Elevation gain: 4150 feet
Hikable: Lower trail, May–October; summit, July–October
Use: Light
Maps: Green Trails No. 144 Bench Mark Mtn., No. 145 Wenatchee Lake; USGS Mount Howard

Driving directions: Turn off Highway 2 at 8.5 miles east of Stevens Pass, shortly past a highway maintenance station. Park immediately and follow the rough powerline service road up a couple of switchbacks to where the trail can be found near the highest pylon, at about 2700 feet.

Flower-filled meadows, an ice-blue lake, and spectacular summit views are all to be found on Rock Mountain. Two approaches are possible: this south-side route going straight up from Highway 2 and mostly in the sun, and one starting 900 feet higher from Snowy Creek, ascending much of the way through shady forests (see Hike 39).

The south side trail up Rock Mountain is a longer, harder approach than the northwest route from Snowy Creek (see Hike 39), and Ira Spring has been known to go so far as to question the sanity of anyone who would go up this way rather than from Snowy Creek. But the route does have its attractions, and although its nearly full exposure to the sun can make for a hot climb if done at midday, it also means that the snow melts off much earlier than on the Snowy Creek side. It's often possible to hike up to about the 5000-foot level as early as the beginning of May. Watch for ticks in springtime here.

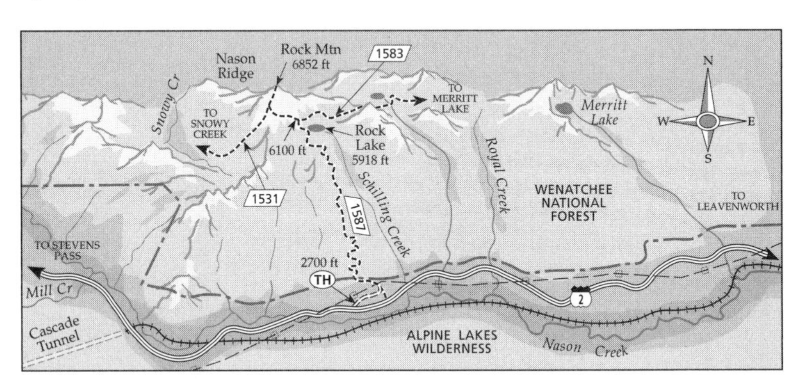

The trail starts out with a series of short switchbacks climbing steadily through a nice woodland of big, old, widely spaced and fire-scorched Douglas firs. A few ponderosa pines can be seen along the lower trail, possibly the westernmost ones in the Highway 2 corridor. The slope that the trail ascends is right in the middle of the transition zone where the wet west and the dry east meet and fight it out, and species from both sides can be seen. Often the west-side clouds can be seen breaking up and dying right here. Periodic fire has played a major role in shaping this woodland, clearing away brush and favoring the growth of grasses. Evidence of it can be seen on many of the trees. Fires are no longer allowed to burn here, though, allowing brush and small trees to invade the grassy spaces between the trees.

Views grow broader as one switchbacks up and up and up. Above 5000 feet, the trail follows a rib up to a 6100-foot junction, where the Nason Ridge trail descends east to deep blue Rock Lake, seen below. The main trail heads up and west, joining the route from Snowy Creek just before reaching the 6852-foot summit of Rock Mountain with its superb views of the entire Central Cascades.

Rock Mountain trail; Chiwaukum Mountains in the distance

41 MERRITT LAKE

Round trip: 7 miles
Hiking time: 3–4 hours
High point: 5000 feet
Elevation gain: 2000 feet
Hikable: June–October
Use: Heavy
Maps: Green Trails No. 145 Wenatchee Lake; USGS Mount Howard, Lake Wenatchee

Driving directions: Drive north from Highway 2 on road 657 about 11.4 miles east of Stevens Pass, 3.3 miles east of a highway maintenance yard. The road is usually signed and reaches the trailhead at its end, in 1.6 miles.

Merritt Lake offers a relatively easy hike to a pretty lake, and the trail can be followed farther to the Alpine Lookout (see Hike 42), which is still occasionally manned and has outstanding views.

The trail starts out by switchbacking up through an open forest of big old Douglas firs and some ponderosa pines. At 2 miles a junction with the Nason Ridge trail is reached; go right another not very steep mile through open forest to Merritt Lake, 5003 feet. Mountain ash and huckleberries make for very nice fall colors here.

For those willing to put up with a bit of brush, it's possible to follow the trail up slopes to the east of the lake, leaving it where it starts traversing east toward Alpine Lookout (Hike 42). Climb through relatively open forest

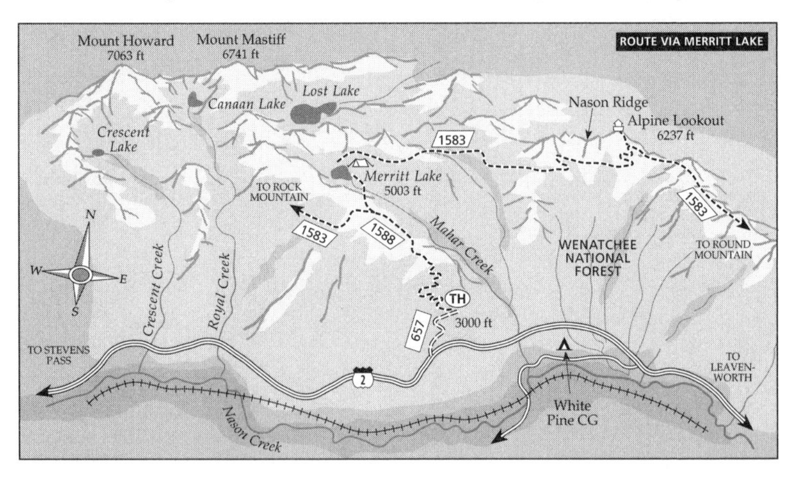

Merritt Lake

to the ridge top north of Merritt Lake. From here, one can look south to the Chiwaukum Mountains and north down to Lost Lake in a cirque far below. This ridge can be followed northwest without much difficulty all the way to the top of Mount Mastiff, 6741 feet, with views in all directions.

Alpine Lookout

Round trip: 12⅘ miles, 10 miles via east route
Hiking time: 6 hours
High point: 6235 feet
Elevation gain: 3235 feet, 2300 feet via east route
Hikable: July–October
Use: Moderate
Maps: Green Trails No. 145 Wenatchee Lake; USGS Mount Howard, Lake Wenatchee

Driving directions: Drive north from Highway 2 on road 657 about 11.4 miles east of Stevens Pass, 3.3 miles east of a highway maintenance yard. The road is usually signed and reaches the trailhead at its end, in 1.6 miles.

Mountain goat at Alpine Lookout

The trail to the Alpine Lookout passes pretty Merritt Lake (Hike 41). The Alpine Lookout, which is still occasionally manned and has outstanding views, can also be reached by a slightly shorter trail from the east.

The trail starts out by switchbacking up through an open forest of big old Douglas firs and some ponderosa pines. At 2 miles a junction with the Nason Ridge trail is reached; go right another not very steep mile through

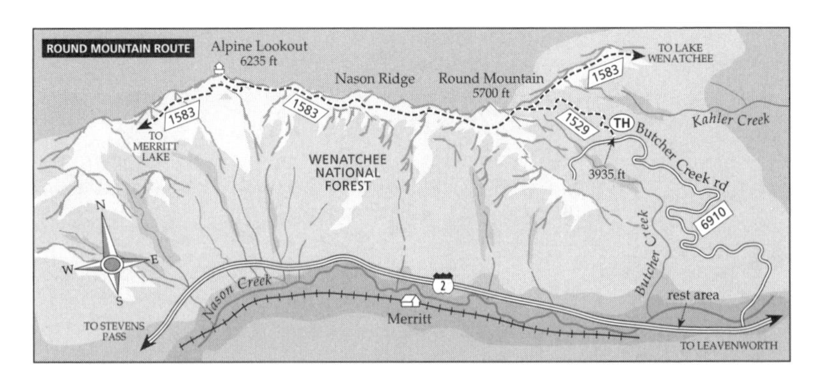

open forest to Merritt Lake, elevation 5003 feet. Mountain ash and huckleberries make for very nice fall colors here.

For the Alpine Lookout, go past the lake and climb a short way to a junction. The left route leads to Lost Lake in a rough and mostly downhill 1.6 miles. Keep right and follow the Nason Ridge trail for almost 3 mostly level miles. A burned area with many interesting snags is passed. About 3 miles from Merritt Lake, go left at a junction and reach the 6235-foot summit in 0.3 mile. Views are all encompassing: the Lake Wenatchee and Glacier Peak country to the north, and all of the eastern Alpine Lakes to the south.

It's also possible to hike to the Alpine Lookout via a slightly shorter 10-mile round trip, with 2300 feet of elevation gain from Round Mountain. Seventeen miles east of Stevens Pass and 0.3 mile east of the Nason Creek rest area, turn north on Butcher Creek road 6910 (unsigned but marked by a row of mailboxes). At 4.6 miles, go right on road (6910)170 for 0.2 mile to the trailhead. The trail traverses some burned areas to the junction with the Nason Ridge trail, at 1.5 miles. Go left. Unfortunately, the Forest Service allows motorcycles on this otherwise attractive ridge-top trail as far as the junction just below the lookout, 5 miles from the road.

CHIWAUKUM CREEK

Round trip: 11 miles
Hiking time: 6–7 hours
High point: 3400 feet
Elevation gain: 1500 feet
Hikable: June–November
Use: Moderate
Maps: Green Trails No. 177 Chiwaukum Mountains; USGS Big Jim Mountain

Driving directions: Drive Highway 2 east of Stevens Pass for 26 miles to the usually signed Chiwaukum Creek road, between mileposts 89 and 90. Turn south (actually southwest) and go 0.3 mile to a gate and trailhead parking. Walk the gated road past some cabins to where it turns to trail.

A low valley walk just off Highway 2 through mostly intact old growth forest.

The trail follows the deep lower valley through moist, mossy forest, with many large Douglas fir trees, a few ponderosa pines, and some cedars. The valley gradually widens and more ponderosa pines can be seen on the south-facing slopes. About 4 miles in, the forest is no longer untouched,

Small meadow along the Chiwaukum Creek trail

this being formerly private land where the big ponderosas were taken out via a road from McCue Ridge to the north. Conservationists tried to get the entire Chiwaukum valley into the Alpine Lakes Wilderness but were unable to save this 1-square-mile section. It has now been added to the national forest, the road has been put to bed, and though the large pines are mostly gone, it's still a worthwhile walk. Real virgin forest is soon

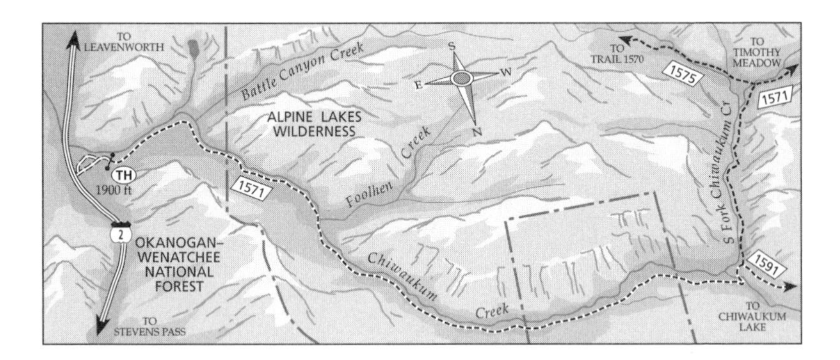

re-entered, and at 5½ miles, 3400 feet, the junction with the South Fork Chiwaukum trail is reached.

Destinations beyond here are mostly outside day-hiking range, with Chiwaukum Lake farther up the main fork, 9.5 miles from the highway. For those who want more, the South Fork is recommended, opening up to a broad valley. Timothy Meadow, at 8 miles from the road, is an attractive destination with grassy flats fringed by aspens. Numerous lakes and mountains lie beyond.

44 TUMWATER PIPELINE TRAIL

Round trip: 2 miles
Hiking time: 1 hour
High point: 1400 feet
Elevation gain: 100 feet
Hikable: Most of the year
Use: Moderate
Maps: Green Trails No. 178 Leavenworth; USGS Leavenworth

Driving directions: From Highway 2 near the bottom of the Tumwater Canyon, about 1.5 miles west of Leavenworth, between mileposts 98 and 99, notice a steel bridge across the river. Just downstream is a parking area below the highway, elevation 1300 feet.

Before 1956 and the adoption of diesel engines, the Great Northern Railway used electric locomotives between Skykomish and Peshastin, since steam engines produced too much exhaust to be used through the Cascade

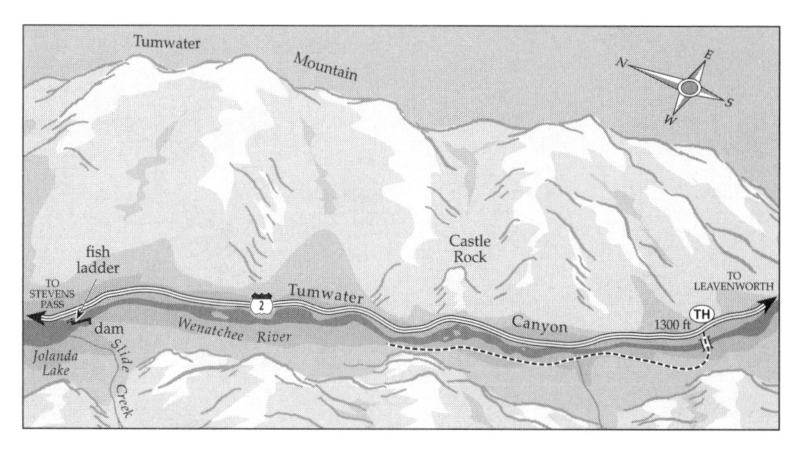

Tunnel. This short walk follows the route of a pipeline that carried water from the Jolanda Lake dam, which can be seen from the highway just below a candy store, to a now-vanished generating plant near the beginning of the trail that supplied power for the electric engines.

Walk upstream a short distance and cross the bridge. On the far side go right, following the old pipeline route upstream. Spring flowers are plentiful from April to June, and the river puts on quite a show during the peak of run-off in June. The riverbank changes from year to year, but there is usually a wide, sandy beach at about ¾ mile. The USGS map shows the trail extending all the way to the dam, but a cliff opposite Castle Rock is an effective end to the walk, except possibly during very low water late in the year.

The Wenatchee River in Tumwater Canyon

45 Icicle Ridge

Round trip: 3 miles
Hiking time: 2–3 hours
High point: 3000 feet
Elevation gain: 1800 feet
Hikable: April–November
Use: Light
Maps: Green Trails No. 178 Leavenworth; USGS Leavenworth

Driving directions: Turn south off Highway 2 at the west end of Leavenworth onto the Icicle Creek road and follow it south 1.4 miles, to where a segment of older road goes off to the right. Turn in and find the Icicle Ridge trailhead, elevation 1200 feet.

The eastern end of the Icicle Ridge trail, the closest trail to Leavenworth, is for some reason only lightly hiked when other trails farther up the Icicle are often mobbed. Although it's a long, dry walk to the high country, the

White-headed woodpecker

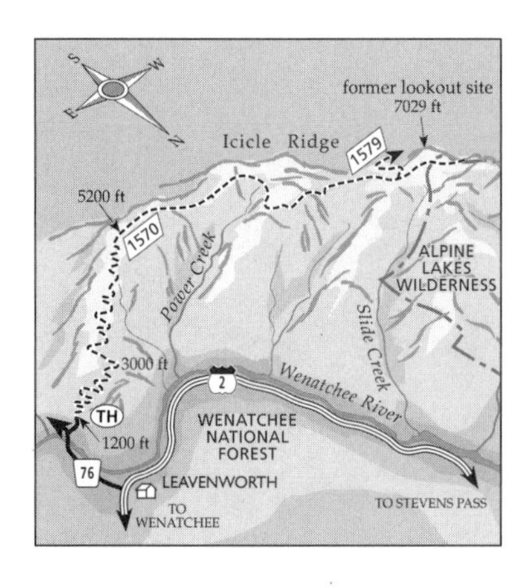

lower trail makes a good day hike up to the northeast shoulder of Icicle Ridge. From time to time a proposal for a tramway here surfaces, which will hopefully never be built.

Decades of fire suppression here prevented the once-frequent light ground fires that kept fuel loads from building up. The stage was thus set for the explosive fires that struck in 1994. Subsequent salvage logging did further damage. The views were improved, though, and the trail starts switchbacking up immediately. The Icicle valley sits below, and Leavenworth can be glimpsed to the north. Spring flowers are abundant. In about 1½ miles, elevation 3000 feet, the shoulder of Icicle Ridge is reached, and the Tumwater Canyon and Highway 2 can be seen far below.

The ridge makes a good turnaround point, although the trail can be followed as far and as high as time, energy, and water supply allow. Views get better, and after 9 miles the junction with the Fourth of July Creek trail and site of the former Icicle Ridge lookout are reached (Hike 51).

46 SNOW CREEK–NADA LAKE

Round trip: 11 miles to Nada Lake
Hiking time: 7–8 hours
High point: 4900 feet
Elevation gain: 3600 feet
Hikable: June–October
Use: Very heavy
Maps: Green Trails No. 209S The Enchantments; USGS Leavenworth, Blewett

Driving directions: The trailhead can be found on the south side of the Icicle Creek road 4 miles from where it turns south off of Highway 2 at the west end of Leavenworth.

The Snow Creek trail is the main access to the Enchantment Lakes Basin, a place that has become so popular that the Forest Service has had to adopt a permit system to control the population explosion that was threatening to destroy the place. While not as overrun as it once was, it's still busy. The

Scenic cascade along the Snow Creek trail

lower trail is a worthy day-hike objective on its own, no permit required, and can be followed to Nada Lake, or even to Snow Lakes for those in good shape who start early.

The trail drops and crosses Icicle Creek on a footbridge, which replaced

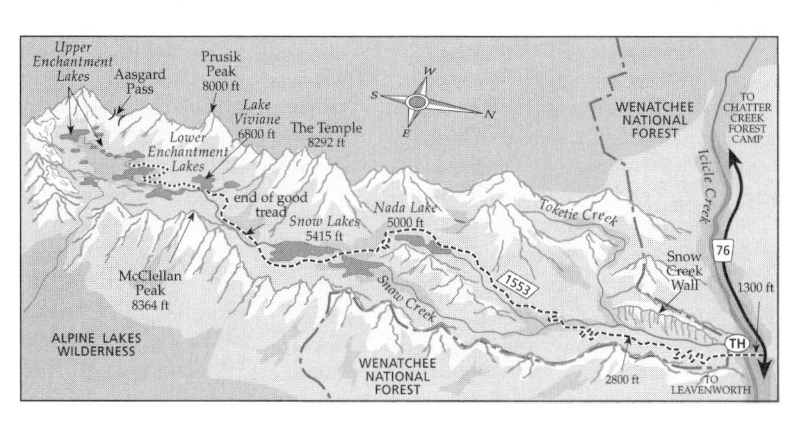

one burned in the 1994 fires, which also burned the forest for about the first 4 miles. It then gains elevation steadily, passing under the cliffs of Snow Creek Wall, where mountain goats can occasionally be seen. More switchbacks follow, the creek is crossed, and after a fairly long 5½ miles, narrow Nada Lake is reached.

Another mile or so and 550 feet of elevation gain brings one to the dam between the more scenic Snow Lakes, nestled below granite cliffs. The upper lake is sometimes drawn down to provide water for the Leavenworth fish hatchery, producing an unattractive bathtub-ring effect. The Enchantment Lakes Basin is another 3 or more miles, out of day-hike range for any but the superhuman.

47 EIGHTMILE LAKE

Round trip: 7 miles
Hiking time: 4–5 hours
High point: 4641 feet
Elevation gain: 1360 feet
Hikable: June–November
Use: Heavy
Maps: Green Trails No. 177 Chiwaukum Mountains; USGS Cashmere Mountain

Driving directions: On the west side of Leavenworth, turn south from Highway 2 onto the Icicle Creek road and follow it 8.5 miles to the Eightmile Creek road 7601. Turn left and drive 3 miles to the Eightmile Creek trailhead, elevation 3280 feet.

Until the early 1970s, Eightmile Lake was a delightful low-to-high walk, starting at Icicle Creek and ascending through a wonderful forest of big "yellowbelly" ponderosa pines, climbing gradually into the mountains, a full day's hike to a good place to camp. But timber was king in the Forest Service, and despite spirited opposition from conservation groups, a road was punched up Eightmile Creek and the pines hauled away. The road was paid for by taxpayers and the pines sold off cheaply. Eightmile Lake is still worth visiting, but the valley below is a painful place for those who remember it "the way it was."

The remnant trail starts out on a now-abandoned road through a forest logged in the 1970s assault, and then burned in 1994. No shade, but early season flowers do offer some consolation. After a long mile, the road enters forest that didn't interest the timber beasts, and at 2½ miles Little Eightmile Lake and a trail junction are reached. The right fork ascends to Lake Caroline (Hike 48). Continue straight ahead for Eightmile Lake,

Eightmile Lake

through a massive reddish rock-slide area, and soon you will reach the destination. In the 1930s, both Eightmile and Little Eightmile were dammed to supply water for irrigation and for the Icicle Creek fish hatchery. As a result, in late season the lake is drained down, leaving an unattractive bathtub-ring effect. It's full and pretty in early summer, though, fringed by

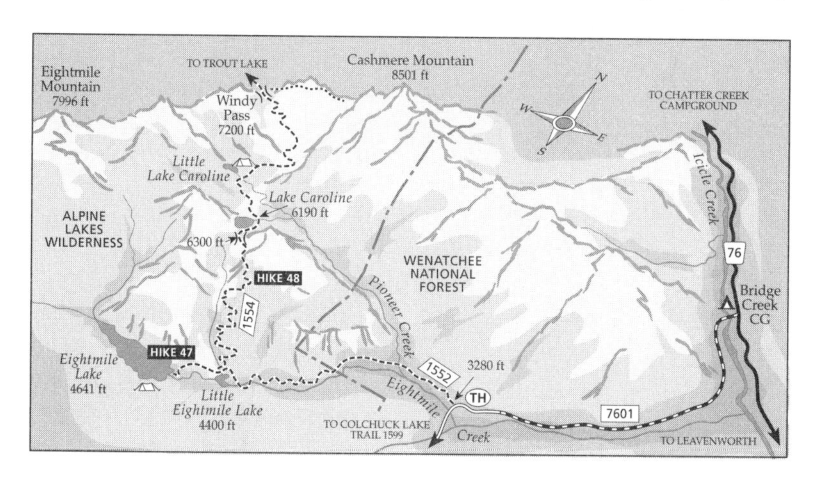

trees, with views of steep Jack Ridge and Eightmile Mountain beyond. Special Enchantment Lakes permits are required for overnight camping; check with the Leavenworth Ranger Station for availability.

48 LAKE CAROLINE

Round trip: 11 miles
Hiking time: 8 hours
High point: 7200 feet
Elevation gain: 3900 feet
Hikable: July–October
Use: Heavy
Maps: Green Trails No. 177 Chiwaukum Mountains; USGS Cashmere Mountain

Driving directions: On the west side of Leavenworth, turn south from Highway 2 onto the Icicle Creek road and follow it 8.5 miles to the Eightmile Creek road 7601. Turn left and drive 3 miles to the Eightmile Creek trailhead, elevation 3280 feet.

The trail to Lake Caroline starts out on an abandoned road through what was once a beautiful forest of ponderosa pines, logged in a money-losing timber sale in the 1970s and then burned in 1994. About the only good thing resulting from the logging and burning is a profusion of springtime flowers, which soak up the now-abundant sun. After a long first mile the road ends and the real trail begins, and at 2½ miles, Little Eightmile Lake and a trail junction are reached. The straight-ahead option goes to Eightmile Lake (Hike 47) and the right fork to Lake Caroline.

Rosy twisted stalk

For Lake Caroline, turn right and start climbing up and up through mostly burned forest, hot and dry in the sunshine and requiring frequent water breaks. After climbing about 1500 feet above Little Eightmile, delightful meadow country is reached. The trail traverses a small basin, climbs over a

6300-foot saddle, and drops a little more than a hundred feet down to Lake Caroline, a lovely spot.

Things keep getting better, though. The trail continues through meadowlands past Lake Caroline and on up to 7200-foot Windy Pass. Ridges beckon north and south, with spectacular views all around. About the first of October, alpine larches turn flaming gold, an unforgettable sight. Special Enchantment Lakes permits are required for overnight camping; check with the Leavenworth Ranger Station for availability.

Lake Caroline

49 LAKE STUART

Round trip: 10 miles
Hiking time: 7 hours
High point: 5064 feet
Elevation gain: 1600 feet
Hikable: July–October
Use: Heavy
Maps: Green Trails No. 209S The Enchantments; USGS Cashmere Mountain, Enchantment Lakes

Driving directions: From Highway 2 at the west end of Leavenworth, turn south on the Icicle Creek road and drive 8.5 miles to the Eightmile Creek road. Turn left and in 3.8 miles reach the trailhead for Mountaineer Creek.

Hikes 49 and 50 are to two very scenic lakes on the north side of the Stuart Range. Both are even more popular than they are scenic; it would be fair to say that Colchuck is downright crowded, offering as it does an access to the Enchantment Lakes Basin through Aasgard Pass. Lonesomeness vanished here when roads were pushed up Eightmile Creek in the 1970s. Combined, they make for a solid weekend of exploration. Camping is by permit only; check with the Leavenworth Forest Service office for availability.

The Mountaineer Creek trail starts out and keeps to a steady uphill grade, climbing through forest to reach a junction at 2½ miles, 4500 feet. The left fork climbs to Colchuck Lake (Hike 50). Go straight ahead for Lake

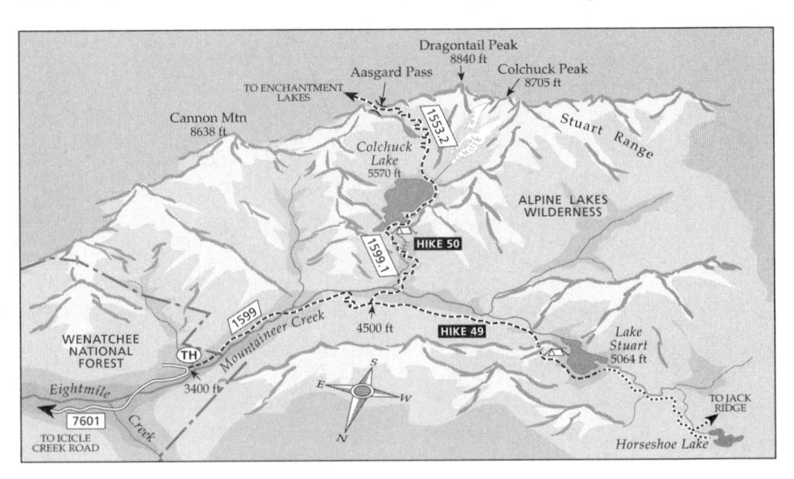

Stuart, passing a couple of interesting marshy areas. At 5 miles, 5064 feet, the lake is reached. A gentle, semiforested knoll to the northwest has some views up to Mount Stuart and its disappearing glaciers. Views are even better from a marshy basin beyond the lake, tucked under the mass of Stuart.

Lake Stuart and Mount Stuart, right, in the Alpine Lakes Wilderness

50 COLCHUCK LAKE

Round trip: 9 miles
Hiking time: 6–7 hours
High point: 5570 feet
Elevation gain: 2140 feet
Hikable: July–October
Use: Very heavy
Maps: Green Trails No. 209S The Enchantments; USGS Cashmere Mountain, Enchantment Lakes

Driving directions: From Highway 2 at the west end of Leavenworth, turn south on the Icicle Creek road and drive 8.5 miles to the Eightmile Creek road. Turn left and in 3.8 miles reach the trailhead for Mountaineer Creek.

Colchuck Lake was once protected by 10 miles of trail, some of which passed through some of the most beautiful ponderosa pine forest in the entire Wenatchee country. But in the 1970s, the Forest Service pushed a road up Eightmile Creek and laid out a money-losing timber sale, destroying the forests and dramatically shortening the hike to Colchuck Lake, which is now a contender for the title of most crowded place in the Cascades.

The Mountaineer Creek trail starts immediately uphill and climbs steadily through forest to a junction at 2½ miles, 4500 feet. The right fork goes to Lake Stuart (Hike 49).

Yum, yum—blueberries

For Colchuck Lake, go left and climb through forest and rock outcrops to the 5570-foot lake, which late in the year is drawn down to supply water to the Icicle Creek fish hatchery. The dark mass of Dragontail Peak looms broodingly above the far end of the lake, with remnants of the fast-disappearing Colchuck Glacier withering away to the right. Camping is by permit only; check with the Leavenworth Ranger Station for availability.

To the left of Dragontail, a steep but heavily boot-beaten path ascends to Aasgard Pass, once regarded as a back-door way into the Enchantment Lakes Basin. But the "back-door" days are long gone. Joel Connelly, veteran outdoor chronicler and writer for the *Seattle Post-Intelligencer,* once wrote that when sitting above Aasgard and looking down at the steady stream of people threading their way up the route from Colchuck, they looked to him like a "more colorful" version of Marshal Tito's partisan army marching en masse up a pass in the mountains of Yugoslavia during World War II.

Don't expect any solitude here. The Cascades have thousands of square miles of terrain where a person could go for decades without seeing another soul and die from loneliness. But not here. Colchuck Lake and the Enchantment Lakes Basin are no doubt beautiful areas, but it's one of nature's more profound mysteries why 95 percent of hikers seem to go to only 5 percent of the places.

Beaver pond along the Mountaineer Creek trail

51 FOURTH OF JULY CREEK–ICICLE RIDGE

Round trip: 12 miles
Hiking time: 8 hours
High point: 7000 feet
Elevation gain: 4800 feet
Hikable: April–October
Use: Moderate
Maps: Green Trails No. 177 Chiwaukum Mountains; USGS Cashmere Mountain

Driving directions: From Highway 2 on the west side of Leavenworth, drive south on the Icicle Creek road 9.4 miles to a small paved parking area at the Fourth of July trailhead, elevation 2250 feet.

A route to a former lookout site that climbs up—a long way up—a southwest-facing slope, the lower parts of which melt free very early in the season. Come here in spring for a floral display and a hike partway up, or in summer for the complete trip with expansive ridge-top views. Almost 5000 feet of climbing keeps this place from getting too crowded.

The trail starts out climbing through a woodland of big ponderosa pines and Douglas firs, with grassy, flowery openings between the well-spaced trees. "Salvage" logging following burns has claimed many of the best trees in the Icicle valley. The large yellow flowers of balsamroot, or "mule's ears" (a reference to the leaves), are plentiful in May. Glacier lilies can be seen earlier, lupines later. Ponderosa pines grow fewer as one ascends, replaced mostly by Douglas firs. The short switchbacks seem numberless.

At about 5400 feet, there may be water early in the year, but don't count

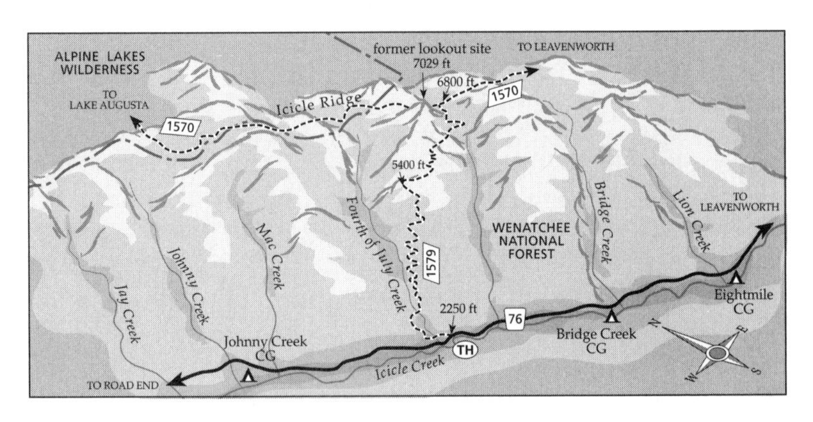

Mount Stuart Range from the Icicle Ridge trail

on it. Views grow broader, dominated by Cashmere Mountain right across the Icicle valley and Stuart beyond. The forest is left behind, and at long last the top of Icicle Ridge is gained. Columbia plateau wheat fields can be seen shimmering in the distance. Icicle Creek to the west, and the Tumwater Canyon to the east, seem infinitely far below; there's a definite sense of height here. A former lookout site was about a quarter of a mile west, atop a big flat boulder, elevation 7029 feet.

It's also possible to hike the Icicle Ridge trail to here from its east end, about 1.4 miles south of Highway 2 on the Icicle Creek road (Hike 45).

52 Icicle Gorge

Loop trip: 4 miles
Hiking time: 2 hours
High point: 2800 feet
Elevation gain: 100 feet
Hikable: April–November
Use: Light
Map: Green Trails No. 177 Chiwaukum Mountains

Driving directions: Drive the Icicle Creek road 15.8 miles from Highway 2 west of Leavenworth, turning left into a large parking lot and the trailhead about 0.5 mile beyond Chatter Creek Campground, elevation 2700 feet. The trail can be hiked in either direction. The left option is described here, which saves the best part for last.

A loop trail goes up one side and down the other side of this section of Icicle Creek, a pleasant short walk partly beside the creek and partly on promontories above the narrow canyon.

The trail follows Icicle Creek downstream along a wide, shallow stretch. Within ¼ mile the creek narrows and picks up speed. At ½ mile, cross a footbridge to the south side. The next couple of miles were selectively logged some years ago, and the trail follows the creek upstream, with several short spurs to bluffs above the water. Eventually the trail re-enters forest and then crosses back to the north side on a concrete road bridge near Rock Island Campground. From here it follows Icicle Creek back downstream, at one point climbing over a rocky promontory above a tight canyon, a good place to sit and enjoy. Below here the creek widens as the trail returns to the starting point.

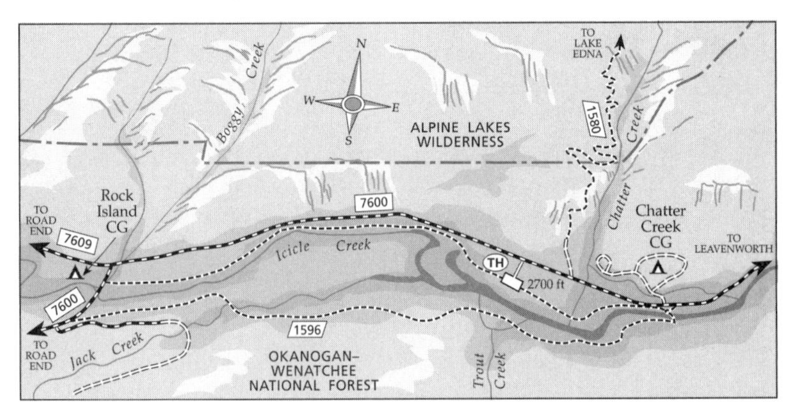

Footbridge over Icicle Gorge

53 CHATTER CREEK–LAKE EDNA

Round trip to Chatter Creek Basin: 5 miles
Hiking time: 3 hours
High point: 5300 feet
Elevation gain: 2500 feet
Hikable: July–October
Use: Moderate

Round trip to Lake Edna: 11½ miles
Hiking time: 8 hours
High point: 6750 feet
Elevation gain: 4500 feet
Hikable: mid-July–September
Use: Moderate

Maps: Green Trails No. 177 Chiwaukum Mountains; USGS Jack Ridge, Chiwaukum Mountains

Driving directions: From Highway 2 west of Leavenworth, drive the Icicle Creek road 15.6 miles, about 0.5 mile past the Chatter Creek Campground, to a side road leading 0.1 mile to the Chatter Creek trail, elevation 2800 feet.

Indian paintbrush

Legend has it that the female names of the lakes in this part of the Cascades refer to the multiple wives of Brigham Young, hence the name "Mormon" Lakes. The Chatter Creek trail climbs from the Icicle valley into a pleasant mountain basin, a good day-hike destination, or it can be followed over a high ridge and then down and back up to scenic Lake Edna for a backpack excursion.

The trail begins in an area logged some years ago, and then starts switchbacking up a hillside of open Douglas fir forest, which gradually steepens. At about 1¼ miles, elevation 4400 feet, cross unbridged Chatter Creek (usually not difficult

Lake Edna

after most of the snow is gone) and then continue climbing along the right side of the creek into the relatively open and level Chatter Creek Basin, a good place for exploration. Campsites can be found, and views look south to Blackjack Ridge, Jack Creek valley, and Eightmile and Cashmere Mountains.

The trail can be followed up and over a 6650-foot shoulder of Grindstone Mountain and then down into the meadowy Index Creek Basin to a junction with the Index Creek trail. Go left and follow tread (which may be faint) up an open rib to 6730-foot, starkly beautiful Lake Edna. Even broader views can be had from the ridge top above.

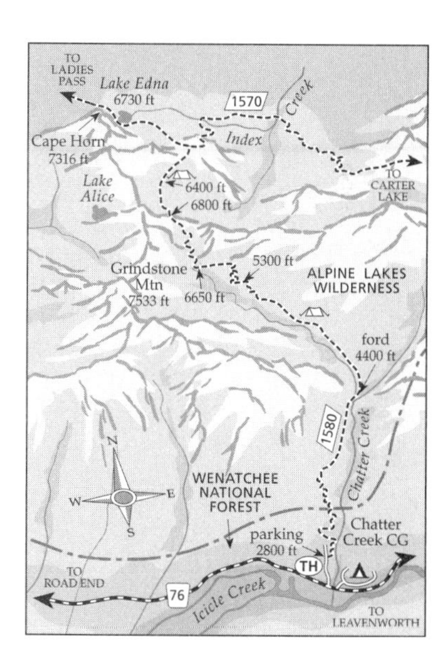

Blackjack Ridge

Round trip: 6 miles to meadows
Hiking time: 5 hours
High point: 6320 feet
Elevation gain: 3400 feet
Hikable: July–September
Use: Light
Maps: Green Trails No. 177 Chiwaukum Mountains; USGS Jack Ridge

Driving directions: From Highway 2 west of Leavenworth, drive Icicle Creek road 18 miles to the Black Pine Campground and horse loading area. Find the Black Pine trail, which parallels the Icicle Creek road heading east.

Mountain daisy

A trail, lightly used because of its steepness, climbing to meadows and superb views over the Icicle valley to Grindstone Mountain, Cashmere, and Stuart. Additional lonely miles can be explored to the south.

About 500 feet down the Black Pine trail, the Blackjack Ridge trail takes off to the right and immediately starts climbing through forest, and keeps climbing for a long 2¾ miles to where it emerges into meadows and views at 6300 feet on a northern shoulder of Bootjack

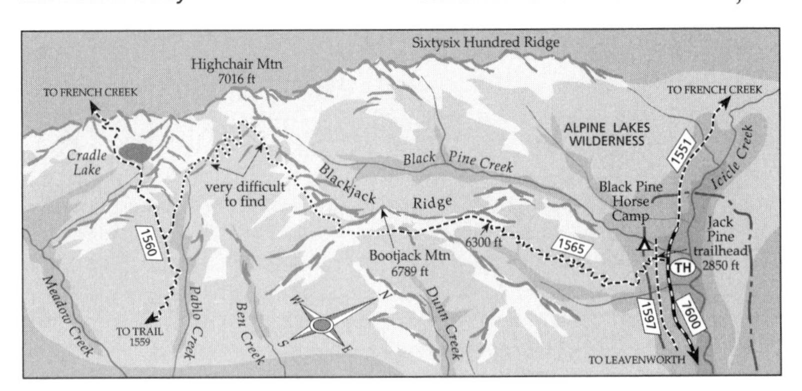

Icicle Creek valley from Blackjack Ridge

Mountain. A flower-filled basin lies immediately below to the south, and views across the deep valley of Jack Creek southeast to the Stuart Range are superb. Bring plenty of water; the basin below is usually dry.

Some maps show a trail heading farther south across the east ridge of Bootjack Mountain, and traces of it can be found in the Ben and Pablo Creek Basins, eventually joining trail 1560 from Meadow Creek to Cradle Lake. This should be considered an off-trail route, and most day hikers will be content with the views and meadows north of Bootjack.

55 Icicle Creek–French Creek Camp

Round trip: 3 miles
Hiking time: 2 hours
High point: 2950 feet
Elevation gain: 50 feet
Hikable: April–November
Use: Heavy
Maps: Green Trails No. 177 Chiwaukum Mountains; USGS Jack Ridge, Chiwaukum Mountains

Driving directions: From Highway 2 west of Leavenworth, drive the Icicle Creek road 17.5 miles. At the Rock Island Campground go left, cross Icicle Creek on a concrete bridge, and follow road 7600 another 1.9 miles to its end, elevation 2900 feet.

The Icicle Creek road does eventually come to an end, with virgin forest and wild country beyond. The Icicle trail is the gateway to a dozen or more backpacks in the Alpine Lakes Wilderness and can be followed for many

French Creek bridge

miles or for just a few. The lower trail is an easy, popular walk through big trees and along a pleasant river.

Along the trail, the Alpine Lakes Wilderness is entered in a few feet, and the trail heads upvalley through splendid ancient forest. French Creek camp, a well-used spot, is reached in about 1¼ miles, a good place for those hiking with small children or just wanting a nice forest and river stroll.

More day-hike possibilities await, with the Icicle Creek trail continuing through many more miles of forest, sometimes close to the creek. The French Creek trail can also be followed as far as time permits, or one can climb the French Ridge trail about 3 waterless miles to the site of a former lookout, with expansive views of the entire eastern Alpine Lakes country.

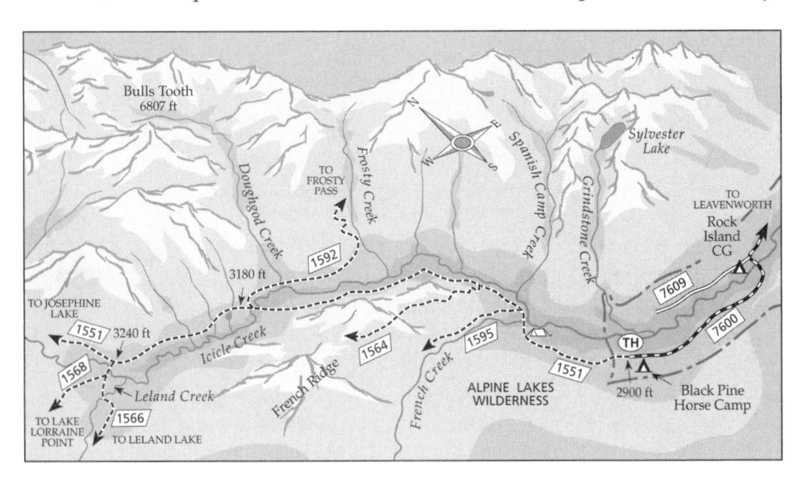

1 TROUBLESOME CREEK

Round trip: ½ mile
Hiking time: 20–40 minutes
High point: 1300 feet
Elevation gain: Slight
Hikable: April–November
Use: Moderate
Maps: Green Trails No. 143 Monte Cristo; USGS Monte Cristo

Driving directions: Drive Highway 2 to the Index turnoff and then go north on the Index–Galena road (also known as the North Fork road) about 11.2 miles to a parking area just outside the Troublesome Creek Campground. If the campground is closed, park outside the gate and walk in, left toward the creek. The trail starts out from the east end of the parking area and can be hiked in either direction. The "clockwise" option is described here.

The clear blue-green waters of Troublesome Creek flow out of one of the few totally untouched valleys in the Wild Sky country, coloring the entire North Fork Skykomish. The creek flows from high mountain lakes, including azure Blanca Lake (Hike 10), which is in turn fed by the Columbia Glacier, source of the striking color that is noticeable even down at Index. A loop trail, perhaps the most attractive short walk in the Wild Sky country, circles an interesting rock gorge in the lower valley.

Turn left at the first trail junction. The trail heads north along the west side of Troublesome Creek, passes under the road bridge, and goes into a forest of tall Douglas fir. After a minute or two a viewpoint is reached of a narrow slot gorge with foaming white falls and green pools.

Spend some time here and if you're lucky you might see a steelhead or a bull trout trying to ascend this impossible-looking mountain of water. If you're very patient and very lucky, you might see one actually make it. Anadromous fish manage to swim all the way here from Puget Sound and up and over these falls to spawn in Troublesome Creek. Late summer and midwinter are the best times to look. If enacted, the Wild Sky Wilderness bill will protect almost 25 miles of spawning grounds here and elsewhere—a first for the Cascades.

The trail continues to a wooden bridge spanning the upper end of the gorge. Across it on the east side a short spur trail goes upstream to some

Troublesome Creek

Douglas fir trees that are visibly bigger than the rest. These trees survived a fire in about the year 1830, which gave rise to the younger surrounding forest. The main trail loops back down the east side of the creek, under the road bridge, and back across the creek on another footbridge to the starting point. Most of the trees east of the creek are noticeably smaller than those on the west side. The trees west of the creek are on better sites, allowing them to grow substantially larger than their neighbors even though they are all about 170 years old.

2 Bear Mountain Viewpoint

Round trip: 1.5 miles
Hiking time: 1 hour
High point: 2800 feet
Elevation gain: 250
Hikable: May–November
Use: Light
Maps: Green Trails No. 143 Monte Cristo; USGS Blanca Lake, Evergreen Mountain

Driving directions: From Highway 2, turn north at the Index turnoff and follow the Index–Galena road (also known as the North Fork road) 14.8 miles north to pavement's end at a four-way junction. Go straight ahead on road 65, cross the North Fork, and climb 2.5 miles to where the road tops out at a five-way intersection at Jack Pass. It's also possible to arrive here by driving up the Beckler road 65 from Highway 2 about a mile east of Skykomish, 13 miles north to the pass. From Jack Pass, climb southeast on road 6570, going 0.6 mile to the first road on the right, unmarked (6570)110, and park.

A short walk to good views on an old logging spur, one of the many kept pointlessly open while badly in need of decommissioning. There is a rough spot right at the beginning that will stop many cars, but it is still drivable and is included here as a "hike-to-be."

A ¾-mile walk up leads to a viewpoint looking northeast up the North

Bear Mountain

Fork valley, with a corridor of old growth forest (the "Hubbard Grove") visible along the river. Directly across north and northwest is Troublesome Mountain. Those who make it here in the winter with a scope or binoculars can look for mountain goats. They can sometimes be seen where steep, south-facing slopes shed snow on Troublesome, exposing forage plants.

Farther on, the road swings around San Juan Ridge and ends in the valley of San Juan Creek. Close across to the west are the fiercely brushy and rocky slopes of Bear Mountain, so rugged that it was not climbed until 1957, and since then approached only by the very few without sense enough to stay off it.

3 LAKE ELIZABETH

Round trip: 7/10 mile
Hiking time: 1 hour
High point: 2900 feet
Elevation gain: None
Hikable: May–November
Use: Light
Maps: Green Trails No. 174 Mount Si; USGS Devils Slide

Driving directions: Drive Highway 2 toward Stevens Pass, and between mileposts 45 and 46, turn right at the sign for "Money Creek Campground." Cross the river on the Old Cascade Highway, pass a campground, and cross the railroad tracks. About a mile from Highway 2, go right on the Miller River road 6410 and in 0.1 mile right again, onto Money Creek road 6420. The road starts out in second growth forest before breaking out into a scenic mountain valley, with old growth forests on the slopes and views south up into Goat Basin and Lennox Mountain. In about 7 miles the lake is reached.

A small mountain lake encircled by trail, only steps away from the Money Creek road. The drive up the scenic Money Creek valley is perhaps more of an attraction than the trail itself, and the road makes a good ski destination when snow covered.

It may take a bit of looking to find the trail. Either way around the lake will work, and some marshy and brushy areas are crossed.

Just past Lake Elizabeth, the road crosses a gentle pass. Shortly before ending, the road enters the South Fork Tolt watershed, which supplies water to Seattle and neighboring cities. The watershed is closed to public entry with the exception of this small section. Several old mines operated in this area many decades ago, and acid drainage from these led the Forest Service in 1980 to describe parts of upper Money Creek as "biologically dead." The lower reaches have recovered somewhat and are now a major spawning area for Chinook and other salmon. A proposal has recently surfaced to reopen the Apex and Damon mines, an economically dubious scheme that threatens not only Money Creek but the Tolt watershed as well, since the Damon mine is on the Tolt side of the divide. Often the true motivation for schemes such as this is not to mine minerals—virtually no mine in the Cascades has ever made a profit, especially not in recent decades—but to drive up the price of the claims in the hope that the Forest Service will buy them out.

Lake Elizabeth

EVANS LAKE

Round trip: 1 mile
Hiking time: 1 hour or less
High point: 3700 feet
Elevation gain: 50 feet
Hikable: June–October
Use: Light
Maps: Green Trails No. 175 Skykomish; USGS Skykomish

Driving directions: Take the Foss River road south from Highway 2 about 1.8 miles east of Skykomish. Follow it past the turnoffs for Tonga Ridge, at 3.6 miles, and Trout Lake, at 4.5 miles. Keep straight ahead on road 68, cross the West Fork Foss bridge, and start climbing. At 8 miles go left on road 6846, which appears to be the main road, and continue another 2 miles to the trailhead sign and parking area at 10.6 miles from the highway, elevation 3650 feet.

Evans Lake

An easy walk to a forest-surrounded lake high on Maloney Ridge, just inside the Alpine Lakes Wilderness. While there are no views from the trail or lake, the upper part of the road has views galore, though trees growing in old clearcuts are gradually closing them off. The trail enters dark, silent hemlock and silver fir forest immediately, crossing the Alpine Lakes Wilderness boundary in a few feet. Soon the lake is reached, and the official trail ends. A brushy way-trail extends around the lake, with possible campsites on the far shore.

Chipmunk having a feast

It's easy to see why upper-elevation old growth forests such as the one surrounding Evans Lake prompted some early explorers to describe them as "gloomy," although the more romantically inclined might use the word "mysterious" instead. Little light penetrates through the canopy of tall hemlock and silver fir trees, and generally the only sound is of silence. Still, these forests have a beauty of their own. Varied thrushes, or "mountain robins," can be heard calling in late spring, a single, plaintive, trilling note that seems to be heard most often on those dark days when the clouds brush right up against the treetops.

5 DECEPTION FALLS NATURE TRAIL

Round trip: ½ mile
Hiking time: 20 minutes
High point: 1800 feet
Elevation gain: Slight
Hikable: April–November
Use: Heavy
Map: Posted at trailhead

Driving directions: The well-marked trail is on the north side of Highway 2, 8 miles east of Skykomish. A short segment of barrier-free trail goes to Deception Creek.

A nice short loop walk through old growth forest with several overlooks of foaming whitewater in Deception Creek and the Tye River. A good place for a break from driving.

The loop path can be walked in either direction, and signs describe natural features along the way. The barrier-free sections descend from the parking lot, with one branch going to an overlook of Deception Creek and the other crossing Deception Creek on a steel bridge. From here a stairway climbs under the highway to a spectacular, noisy, head-on view of the falls, only feet away.

Narrow gorge on the Tye River

6 Bygone Byways

Loop trip: ½ mile
Hiking time: 30 minutes
High point: 3000 feet
Elevation gain: 50 feet
Hikable: May–November
Use: Moderate
Map: On trailhead display sign

Driving directions: The trail can be accessed only from the westbound lanes of this divided section of Highway 2. From Stevens Pass, head east about 6 miles, and just beyond the signs for the Stevens Pass Nordic Area, turn left and descend a short road to turn left again, onto the westbound lanes. The parking area for the trail is a little over 1 mile back to the west.

A short loop walk to portions of the original Stevens Pass "tote road," a wagon road built to carry supplies for railroad builders, and a section of the original railroad bed, which was abandoned after completion of the second Cascade Tunnel in 1929.

Hiker on the Bygone Byways trail

A wide trail drops a few feet to a display detailing some of the history behind these early travel routes across the Cascades. The path goes by the collapsed remnants of an oven used to bake bread for the railroad workers. Parts of three different old "byways" can be seen: the original wagon road, the old railroad bed, and the first automobile road. One particularly impressive section blasted out of rock cliffs above Nason Creek is worth seeing.

7 HIDDEN LAKE

Round trip: 1 mile
Hiking time: 1 hour
High point: 2300 feet
Elevation gain: 350 feet
Hikable: June–November
Use: Moderate
Maps: Green Trails No. 145 Wenatchee Lake; USGS Lake Wenatchee

Driving directions: Twenty miles east of Stevens Pass, turn north on Highway 207 and turn left in 4 miles toward Lake Wenatchee State Park. Go left again shortly onto the South Shore road 6607. Just before

Hidden Lake

the end of the road, find the parking lot and trailhead, at 1950 feet.

A steep but very short hike to a pretty lake surrounded by rounded boulders on three sides.

The well-used trail heads directly up to the lake. Some glimpses can be had out through the trees to Lake Wenatchee and Dirtyface Mountain beyond. Pileated woodpeckers can sometimes be seen here. Hidden Lake is quickly reached at a big sloping rock, which makes a good spot to swim from in warm weather. Find your favorite spot and enjoy.

Clark's nutcracker, commonly known as a camp robber

8 TUMWATER BOTANIC AREA AND ROAD 7903

Round trip: 1 mile to best flowers, 4 miles to ridge
Hiking time: ½ hour to flowers, 2 hours to ridge
High point: 3200 feet at ridge
Elevation gain: 500 feet, 1600 feet to ridge top
Hikable: April–November
Use: Light
Maps: Green Trails No. 179 Leavenworth; USGS Winton

Driving directions: Drive Highway 2 from Stevens Pass toward Leavenworth, past Tumwater Campground and just south of the Swift Water Picnic Area. Look for road 7903 on the left (east), 0.2 mile past milepost 92. Park near the gate, elevation 1640 feet.

The Tumwater Canyon is one of the scenic highlights of Highway 2 and a good place for early season flowers, when the high country is buried under many feet of snow. A surprising number of species often thought of as alpine can be seen in east-side forests in early spring, along with many that grow only in low forests. This is also a place where you might encounter the elusive *Lewisia tweedyi,* a flower so uncommon that it has no common name. There aren't many trails in the Tumwater Canyon, but gated road 7903 is a pleasant and usually pretty dependable flower walk.

Just what the floral display will be depends on the date, recent weather,

Lewisia tweedyi

and slope aspect. Glacier lily emerges as early as the end of March some years. These are followed in April by trillium, spring beauty, and very orange-tinted paintbrush. Lupine usually starts blooming toward the end of April or early May. Bright yellow balsamroot is plentiful in more open areas.

Look for *Lewisia tweedyi* in rocky areas along the first ½ mile of road. The semisucculent leaf bunches can vaguely resemble a smaller version of balsamroot leaves, and the showy flowers are creamy white, sometimes trending to pink. Don't disturb them. Road 7903 climbs through areas where most of the big trees have been logged, but it is still a worthwhile walk up to open, grassy hillsides. A number of spurs lead to various high points on Tumwater Ridge, some with views west to Josephine Crag, Icicle Ridge, and Big Jim Mountain.

9 CASTLE ROCK

Round trip: ½ mile
Hiking time: 15–20 minutes
High point: 1800 feet
Elevation gain: 400 feet
Hikable: Usually all year
Use: Moderate
Map: Green Trails No. 178 Leavenworth, USGS Leavenworth

Driving directions: Follow Highway 2 to near the bottom of the Tumwater Canyon, to a point about halfway between mileposts 97 and 98, where a wide parking area can be found just below the bulk of Castle Rock.

Castle Rock has been a popular practice spot for rock climbers for many years. A trail constructed for their benefit is a worthwhile short walk in itself. From the parking area, the trail switchbacks up along the north side

Castle Rock and the Wenatchee River in Tumwater Canyon

of the rock to a viewpoint looking down some 200 or so feet to the highway and river. From there it continues on up to broader views from the top of Castle Rock, with the Wenatchee River below. Trees on the opposite slope were blackened in 1994 fires and are now slowly regreening.

Peregrine falcons sometimes nest on the rock face, and signs request climbers to avoid them in season. A variety of flowers can be viewed in the surrounding forest in spring, and bigleaf maple trees grow near the bottom of the trail. Bigleaf maples are usually thought of as a west-side species, but small numbers of them can be found in the Tumwater Canyon and nearby areas. It's a wonder how such lush-looking trees manage to find enough water to survive the dry summers here.

10 PESHASTIN PINNACLES

Round trip: 1½ miles
Hiking time: 45 minutes
High point: 1500 feet
Elevation gain: 450 feet
Hikable: Most of the year
Use: Moderate
Map: Posted on reader board at parking area

Driving directions: Turn north off Highway 2 just short of milepost 109, where signs show the way to Peshastin Pinnacles State Park. The parking lot is about 0.4 mile from the highway, elevation approximately 1050 feet.

Balsamroot

The Peshastin Pinnacles (also sometimes called the Cashmere Crags, because they are much closer to Cashmere than Peshastin) stand out prominently to the north as one drives Highway 2 between Dryden and Cashmere. Used primarily for rock climbing, they are also a good place to take a springtime flower walk and watch climbers practice their skills.

The State Parks people have built a series of trails that switchback up to and among the various

Peshastin Pinnacles

pinnacles. Any of them will do as a way to go up the hillside, where views open up to the fruit orchards below and across the Wenatchee valley to pine-dotted hills to the south. Several loops allow circuits to be walked. Many 15- to 20-foot-tall, multitrunked serviceberry shrub/trees can be seen, with fragrant white blossoms in late April and delicious berries usually in June. Herbaceous flowers put on a spring show, too, with the big yellow sunflowerlike blossoms of balsamroot blooming in April most years, followed by blue lupines in May. Yellow bells, buckwheats, delphiniums, and penstemons can sometimes be seen, as well as the onionlike flowers of death camas. The apple orchards bloom around the first of May, carpeting the valley in foamy white.

SUGGESTED READING

Beckey, Fred. *Cascade Alpine Guide, Climbing and High Routes, Volume 1: Columbia River to Stevens Pass,* 3d ed. Seattle: The Mountaineers Books, 2000.

—. *Cascade Alpine Guide, Climbing and High Routes, Volume 2: Stevens Pass to Rainy Pass,* 2d ed. Seattle: The Mountaineers Books, 2003.

Fred Beckey's *Cascade Alpine Guide* series well deserves the nickname "Beckey's Bibles." They continue on where the hiking guides stop, and are full of useful information about not only mountain climbing and high alpine traverses but also history and geology. All of it is delivered in classic Beckey style—crisp, direct, and to the point—just like the way he climbs mountains. Fascinating for actual and armchair climbers alike.

—. *Range of Glaciers: The Exploration and Survey of the Northern Cascade Range.* Portland: Oregon Historical Society, 2003.

Fred Beckey is famous for making more first ascents in the Cascades than anyone. He's as great a writer as he is a climber, though, and this volume takes the reader on a journey through the history of the Cascades as exciting as one of his first ascents. Beckey has not only searched through musty archives but also explored the places on the ground, making this the definitive work on early Cascade history.

Cameron, David. *An Illustrated History of Snohomish County.* Hamilton, Montana: Oso Publishing Co., 2003.

Longtime Index resident David Cameron has built upon earlier works to produce an engaging, highly readable history of Snohomish County and the people who have shaped it from the beginning to the present, looking not only back but forward as well. Covers Native Americans, early European settlement, homesteading, and mining and logging in the Skykomish valleys.

Spring, Ira and Harvey Manning. *100 Hikes in Washington's Alpine Lakes.* Seattle: The Mountaineers Books, 2000.

—. *100 Hikes in Washington's Glacier Peak Region.* Seattle: The Mountaineers Books, 2003.

The *100 Hikes* series of books by Ira Spring and Harvey Manning is the gold standard of Cascade hiking guides. Imitators abound, but no one has ever surpassed them. Spring has spent most of a lifetime exploring, photographing, and protecting trails in the Cascades, and Manning has been at the center of efforts to protect the lands and forests of the Cascades since the 1950s. Manning's wit and humor make the series not only useful but fun to read, too. The Alpine Lakes volume covers country south of Highway 2; the Glacier Peak volume covers areas to the north. Rely on these for information on longer, deeper trips into the wilderness beyond the day-hike emphasis of this book.

INDEX

ABOUT THE AUTHOR AND PHOTOGRAPHER

RICK McGUIRE

Rick McGuire developed an interest in the forests of the Cascades as a high school student in Everett, Washington. He currently serves as a volunteer conservationist on the boards of the Alpine Lakes Protection Society and the North Cascade Conservation Council. His main interest at present is protecting old growth and second growth forests in the Skykomish and Middle Fork Snoqualmie valleys.

IRA SPRING

A master hiker, photographer, and author, Ira Spring is considered the father of Pacific Northwest hiking books, with more than twenty-five titles to his credit, including *100 Classic Hikes in Washington* (with co-author Harvey Manning) and *An Ice Axe, A Camera, and a Jar of Peanut Butter* (his autobiography). He devotes much of his time to organizations advocating trail and wildlife preservation. Spring was co-founder of the Washington Trails Association and received the Theodore Roosevelt Conservation Award in 1992.

THE SPRING FAMILY TRAIL FUND

Established in 2000 by well-known outdoor photographer and author Ira Spring, The Spring Family Trail Fund is a nonprofit organization dedicated to keeping hiking trails open for this and future generations of hikers in the state of Washington. The organization collects and distributes Spring family funds, including royalties from Spring's books, plus donations from corporations and individuals. Collaborating closely with the Washington Trails Association, these funds are used in supporting volunteer trail maintenance, helping train Certified Trail Crew Leaders, and replacing rotting bridges on popular hiking trails, among other trail-related projects.

As of April 2003, the fund has helped to keep the Granite Creek bridge together (Methow area); has opened up the White River trail (Wenatchee National Forest), which was closed by a flood five years ago; and has paid for a helicopter to lift the Barclay Creek bridge in place and helped the Forest Service finish the Humpback Creek bridge (both in the Interstate 90 corridor), used by some 20,000 hikers a year. To give hikers more options, the fund is paying for locating and designing a new trail up Mail Box Peak (I-90 corridor).

In 2003, with the aid of a $50,000 grant from REI, the fund is forming a five-way partnership for bridges. The partners are:

1. U.S. Forest Service (will provide initial bridge planning and design)
2. REI (will provide funds)
3. IAC (a state agency that will provide assistance with funding)
4. Washington Trails Association (will provide volunteers for creating bridge approaches)
5. The Spring Family Trail Fund (will coordinate and provide funds)

Visit *www.springtrailtrust.org* for more information about The Spring Family Trail Fund.

THE MOUNTAINEERS, founded in 1906, is a nonprofit outdoor activity and conservation club, whose mission is "to explore, study, preserve, and enjoy the natural beauty of the outdoors. . . . " Based in Seattle, Washington, the club is now the third-largest such organization in the United States, with 15,000 members and five branches throughout Washington State.

The Mountaineers sponsors both classes and year-round outdoor activities in the Pacific Northwest, which include hiking, mountain climbing, ski-touring, snowshoeing, bicycling, camping, kayaking and canoeing, nature study, sailing, and adventure travel. The club's conservation division supports environmental causes through educational activities, sponsoring legislation, and presenting informational programs. All club activities are led by skilled, experienced volunteers, who are dedicated to promoting safe and responsible enjoyment and preservation of the outdoors.

If you would like to participate in these organized outdoor activities or the club's programs, consider a membership in The Mountaineers. For information and an application, write or call The Mountaineers, Club Headquarters, 300 Third Avenue West, Seattle, WA 98119; (206) 284-6310.

The Mountaineers Books, an active, nonprofit publishing program of the club, produces guidebooks, instructional texts, historical works, natural history guides, and works on environmental conservation. All books produced by The Mountaineers Books fulfill the club's mission.

Send or call for our catalog of more than 500 outdoor titles:

The Mountaineers Books
1001 SW Klickitat Way, Suite 201
Seattle, WA 98134
(800) 553-4453
mbooks@mountaineersbooks.org
www.mountaineersbooks.org

The Mountaineers Books is proud to be a corporate sponsor of Leave No Trace, whose mission is to promote and inspire responsible outdoor recreation through education, research, and partnerships. The Leave No Trace program is focused specifically on human-powered (nonmotorized) recreation.

Leave No Trace strives to educate visitors about the nature of their recreational impacts, as well as offer techniques to prevent and minimize such impacts. Leave No Trace is best understood as an educational and ethical program, not as a set of rules and regulations.

For more information, visit *www.LNT.org*, or call (800) 332-4100.

OTHER TITLES YOU MIGHT ENJOY FROM THE MOUNTAINEERS BOOKS:

55 Hikes Around Snoqualmie Pass: Mountains to Sound Greenway, *Ira Spring & Harvey Manning*

100 Hikes in Washington's Alpine Lakes, *Vicky Spring, Ira Spring, & Harvey Manning*

Best Loop Hikes: Washington, *Dan Nelson*

Best Old-Growth Forest Hikes: Washington and Oregon Cascades, *John & Diane Cissel*

Best Winter Walks & Hikes: Puget Sound, *Ira Spring & Harvey Manning*

Best Short Hikes in Washington's North Cascades & San Juan Islands, *E. M. Sterling & Ira Spring*

Exploring Washington's Wild Areas: A Guide for Hikers, Backpackers, Climbers, Cross-Country Skiers, & Paddlers, *Marge & Ted Mueller*

Mountain Flowers of the Cascades & Olympics, *Ira Spring & Harvey Manning*

Available at fine bookstores and outdoor stores, by phone at (800) 553-4453 or on the Web at *www.mountaineersbooks.org*

THE MOUNTAINEERS BOOKS